"In *Cambridge Social Ontology* Yannick Slade-Caffarel provides a useful and insightful overview of Lawson's social positioning theory, which is also timely given the recent spike in interest in the field of social ontology. Philosophers will find the comparison between Lawson's views and those of John Searle to be of particular value".

Charlotte Witt, *Professor of Philosophy, University of New Hampshire*

"All those interested in the theory of social facts, in particular researchers in economics and sociology, will find much to reflect upon in this book. Written with exceptional clarity, a conceptual framework, Social Positioning Theory, is presented that, at the level of social ontology, aims to explain the nature of social totalities. In so doing, many of the most challenging topics (emergence, irreducibility, collective intentionality, collective acceptance, trust) are considered and important clarifications are provided. A must read".

André Orléan, *Directeur d'études, L'École des hautes études en sciences sociales, Directeur de recherche, Centre national de la recherche scientifique*

"You could not wish for a more accessible introduction to the recent work of Tony Lawson and the Cambridge Social Ontology Group. Yannick Slade-Caffarel follows a clear path at a gentle pace that builds up a well-rounded, accurate, and easily understood picture of the group's project and its implications".

Dave Elder-Vass, *Honorary Fellow, School of Social Sciences and Humanities, Loughborough University*

"This welcome volume by Yannick Slade-Caffarel provides an excellent entry point to social positioning theory for those not familiar with its ongoing development. The ideas explained here are the focus of the Social Ontology group centred in Cambridge, UK, following on from the critical realist project. By setting out a thoughtful and careful account of social positioning theory for economics this volume will extend the influence of the social ontology project to a wider audience and encourage further debate".

Sheila Dow, *Emeritus Professor of Economics, University of Stirling*

"Slade-Caffarel's introduction to social positioning theory lays out the foundations of a core subject in the Cambridge social ontology project. The book provides a needed examination of ideas central to explaining social stratification and pervasive social inequality".

John B. Davis, *Professor Emeritus of Economics, Marquette University and University of Amsterdam*

"Yannick Slade-Caffarel has not only provided us with an accessible, insightful account of one the major schools of thought at the intersection of social theory and metaphysics, he has done so in a way that brings to life the 30-plus year history of realist social ontology at Cambridge. Slade-Caffarel is perfectly positioned, as it were, to pull off the admirable feat of introducing readers to a still-evolving body of work, as he himself is a long-standing member of the Cambridge Social Ontology Group. Anyone with an interest in social positioning theory, social ontology generally, or Tony Lawson's work most narrowly, will appreciate this important new resource".

Ruth Groff, *Associate Professor, Saint Louis University*

Cambridge Social Ontology

Social ontology is the study of the nature and basic structure of social reality. It is a rapidly growing field at the intersection of philosophy and social science that has the potential to greatly assist social researchers of all kinds.

One of the longest running projects in social ontology has developed over the better part of the last four decades through the work of Tony Lawson and the Cambridge Social Ontology Group. Cambridge social ontology has its origins in an assessment that the widespread explanatory failure of modern mainstream economics, as well as in the social sciences more generally, is due to sustained ontological neglect and the resulting use of research methods that are inappropriate, given the nature of social material. The Cambridge project's aim has been to rectify this neglect through conducting explicit and sustained inquiry into the nature of social material with a view to elaborating an explanatorily powerful conception of social ontology. The result is social positioning theory. This book is an introduction to the key features of social positioning theory, provides context as to the theory's development and illustrates how social positioning theory can clarify the natures of phenomena such as gender and the corporation.

Cambridge Social Ontology is for social scientists, philosophers and all readers interested in gaining a better understanding of the nature of social phenomena.

Yannick Slade-Caffarel is Lecturer in Economics and Philosophy at King's College London, UK. He is also a member of the Cambridge Social Ontology Group and a co-founder of the Social Ontology Research Unit at King's College London.

Economics as Social Theory

Series edited by Tony Lawson

University of Cambridge

Social Theory is experiencing something of a revival within economics. Critical analyses of the particular nature of the subject matter of social studies and of the types of method, categories and modes of explanation that can legitimately be endorsed for the scientific study of social objects, are re-emerging. Economists are again addressing such issues as the relationship between agency and structure, between economy and the rest of society, and between the enquirer and the object of enquiry. There is a renewed interest in elaborating basic categories such as causation, competition, culture, discrimination, evolution, money, need, order, organization, power probability, process, rationality, technology, time, truth, uncertainty, value etc.

The objective for this series is to facilitate this revival further. In contemporary economics the label "theory" has been appropriated by a group that confines itself to largely asocial, ahistorical, mathematical "modelling". Economics as Social Theory thus reclaims the "Theory" label, offering a platform for alternative rigorous, but broader and more critical conceptions of theorizing.

For more information about this series, please visit: www.routledge.com/ Economics-as-Social-Theory/book-series/EAST

Cambridge Social Ontology
An Introduction to Social Positioning Theory

Yannick Slade-Caffarel

Routledge
Taylor & Francis Group

LONDON AND NEW YORK

Designed cover image: Sam Jane Hunt, *Gonville & Caius College in the Snow*, 2023

First published 2024
by Routledge
4 Park Square, Milton Park, Abingdon, Oxon OX14 4RN

and by Routledge
605 Third Avenue, New York, NY 10158

Routledge is an imprint of the Taylor & Francis Group, an informa business

British Library Cataloguing-in-Publication Data
A catalogue record for this book is available from the British Library

ISBN: 978-0-367-62803-1 (hbk)
ISBN: 978-0-367-62802-4 (pbk)
ISBN: 978-1-003-11087-3 (ebk)

DOI: 10.4324/9781003110873

Typeset in Palatino
by Apex CoVantage, LLC

For Sam

Contents

Preface and acknowledgements

My aim, when beginning this project, was to compare the conception of social ontology developed by Tony Lawson and the Cambridge Social Ontology Group with a number of alternative theories. To start, I thought that it would be helpful to draft a chapter briefly setting out the account of social ontology defended in Cambridge. That was seven years ago. In that time, my brief chapter expanded into a doctoral thesis before eventually becoming this book.

At the very beginning of the project, I began attending the meetings of the Cambridge Social Ontology Group. There, I found that the concepts I had become familiar with through reading books and papers were, every Tuesday morning, debated, questioned and, as a result, continuously evolving. It quickly became obvious that an account based on the work I was already familiar with would not accurately capture the current state of the Cambridge conception of social ontology. Moreover, I observed that key developments were being made towards the conception becoming appropriately known as social positioning theory.

At the time, there was no outline available of social positioning theory. So, abandoning the idea of a brief chapter, I set about trying to provide an initial description of the key features of social positioning theory. Once I had produced a piece of work that broadly achieved that aim, it turned out that there really was no more room for the comparisons I had initially aimed to conduct. So, I submitted my early account of social positioning theory as my doctoral thesis. Soon after, I began developing my thesis for publication. That was four years ago.

As I turned to preparing my dissertation for publication, Tony Lawson began writing a paper aimed at providing an outline of social positioning theory. Lawson's paper developed through many hours of discussion on Tuesday mornings and a seemingly endless number of drafts. It became quickly clear to me that, again, the theory was developing and evolving such that the version discussed in my doctoral thesis would not, by the time it was published, be able to best capture the current state of the theory. Lawson's paper, entitled "Social Positioning Theory" was finally published in the *Cambridge Journal of Economics* in 2022.

It was at this point that I finally realised the obvious. It is in fact impossible to capture, in a manner that accurately describes its latest developments, a theory that is continuously evolving. Indeed, the evolution of social positioning theory has continued since the publication of Lawson's paper. Discussion and debate continue every Tuesday morning and new developments to the theory have already occurred.

It is, however, possible to identify significant points in a theory's development and provide an account of the theory as it stands at that point in time. Moreover, it is not only possible but also useful to provide such an account in a way that introduces a new audience to the theory. Lawson's publication of "Social Positioning Theory" is one such significant point in the development of the Cambridge conception of social ontology. So, I have finally stopped trying to provide some all-encompassing outline of social positioning theory. Rather, the aim, in this book, is to provide an introduction to the theory at that point in its evolution with a view to making it accessible to the largest possible number.

It is perhaps useful here to briefly comment on the approach that I have taken to providing such an introduction. In the main body of each chapter, I have sought to present the key features of the theory as concisely and as clearly as possible. While I hope that presenting the theory in this way will be of value to all readers, my focus has been to provide an outline that will be accessible to an audience that is unfamiliar with the theory.

That said, throughout the years that I have dedicated to this project, I have analysed numerous points in time in the development of social positioning theory and have drawn out the distinctive features of the theory in relation to other conceptions of social ontology. So, rather than jettison everything that was not strictly necessary to an introduction, I have, where this provides helpful context and interesting development, included notes that discuss previous formulations of key features of the theory and compare the framework with the conceptions of other key authors in the area of social ontology, most notably John Searle.

These notes aim to provide those who are familiar with the Cambridge social ontology project with context as to the development of the theory over time, drawing links between earlier versions of the theory and the more recent developments accounted for in this book. These notes are also intended to aid those who are perhaps more familiar with other conceptions of social ontology such as Searle's to appreciate points of similarity and difference between such accounts and social positioning theory.

The book, then, is structured as follows. In Chapter 1, I discuss the intellectual and institutional context in which social positioning theory has developed. I provide a brief history of the Cambridge Realist Workshop and the Cambridge Social Ontology Group over the better part of the last four decades. I then consider the links that exist between the Cambridge project and critical realism before situating social positioning theory in relation to approaches in social ontology broadly informed by analytic philosophy and, most importantly, the work of John Searle.

In Chapter 2, I turn to the theory proper, considering those principles that apply generally to the constitution of both social and non-social phenomena. Here, I introduce the building blocks of the theory, namely that phenomena—both social and non-social—are everywhere constituted through the organisation of pre-existing items to form components of totalities. I explain that such totalities, as well as their components, are irreducible to the items out of which they are constituted and stress that totalities of this sort operate through the workings of their components, not down upon them.

In Chapter 3, the focus is on demarcating the type of phenomena whose constitution social positioning theory aims to explain—social phenomena and, specifically, social totalities. I outline how, within the Cambridge social ontology project, the term social is understood and analyse how this definition has developed over time. I consider the sense in which communities are the most basic social totality and explain that the principles of social positioning, which I outline in the remaining chapters, are specifically those of community social positioning.

In Chapter 4, I turn to the nature of community organising structure. I show that the organisational structure of communities takes the form of social positions constituted as packages or sets of rights and obligations that are always matched. I consider the key features of such packages of rights and obligations and discuss how positions of this sort are constituted. I then outline that such positions require collective acceptance and must be underpinned by trust.

Finally, in Chapter 5, I discuss how different items may be allocated to community social positions, are subjected to different sets of rights and obligations and consequently give rise to community components. I consider the nature of the community components that are so formed, stressing key features such as their irreducibility and the sense in which such components have functions. To conclude, I illustrate how the theory can be used to ground accounts of social phenomena such as gender and the corporation.

There are many people without whom I would not have been able to write this book. To start, I would like to thank every member of, visitor to, and anyone otherwise associated with, the Cambridge Social Ontology Group that I have engaged with since I began attending. I will undoubtedly forget many names but these include Carolina Alves, Bahar Araz, Jana Bacevic, Dave Elder-Vass, Simon Deakin, Phil Faulkner, Ruth Groff, Tobias Heuer, Clive Lawson, Tony Lawson, Paul Lewis, Nuno Martins, Josef Mensik, Imko Meyenburg, Jamie Morgan, Helen Mussell, Paulin Nusser, Heikki Patomäki, Stephen Pratten, Antonis Ragkousis, Jochen Runde, Bill Waller, Isabella Weber and Toru Yamamori.

Of that list, I am especially indebted to two people. The first is Stephen Pratten. Steve was my doctoral supervisor, and I am fortunate to now have him as a colleague. I cannot overstate the level of support that he has provided throughout my doctorate and these early years of my academic career. Indeed, it is frightening to think of how many drafts of this project he has read. His advice, even when—particularly early on—I resisted it at first, has never failed to be right. The second is Tony Lawson. I have, over the years, had a lot of questions. And Tony has been unendingly generous in devoting time to discussing the theory with me. I am particularly appreciative to Tony for reading and commenting upon several versions of the manuscript of this book in their entirety, including the penultimate version.

I have been fortunate that from the very start of my PhD I have had the chance to teach various versions of social positioning theory to now many hundreds of undergraduates. These experiences have undoubtedly influenced the introductory aim of this book. The questions asked, comments made and critique provided by the students I have had the chance to teach at King's College London, the University of Cambridge and Sciences Po, Paris, have been invaluable in terms of refining how such a theory can be most effectively explained.

Finally, I would like to thank my family and friends for all of their support. I must mention the fact that for periods of time during the development of this project, I have relied on the hospitality of Catherine Cameron, James Cameron, Juliet May, Olivia Clark, Luke Edwards as well as John, Neil and Narelle Hassell, who have generously had me to stay at their homes. Above all, I am forever grateful to my partner Sam. I dedicate this book to her.

1   The Cambridge social ontology project

For almost 40 years, a sustained programme of research in social ontology has been pursued in Cambridge. This ongoing project, now regularly referred to as Cambridge social ontology, develops today through the research of members and associates of, visitors to, and other contributors critically engaging with, the Cambridge Social Ontology Group. Its aim is "studying in a systematic fashion the *basic nature and structure of social reality*" (Lawson, 2019b, p. 3).

The project's origins lie in an assessment of the widespread explanatory failure of the modern mainstream of economics. The problem identified is that the ontological presuppositions of the dominant methodological approach employed by the mainstream of economics—mathematical modelling—are inconsistent with the nature of social material. As these methods presuppose a conception of social reality that is demonstrably unrealistic—a world of isolated atoms—it is argued that the contributions provided through their use will likely be irrelevant. To have a chance at producing powerful explanations, one must employ methods that are consistent with the nature of the phenomena studied. And to inform such methodological choices, one must have some idea of the nature of the phenomena one seeks to explain. Social ontology—the study of the nature and basic structure of social reality—is therefore central to successful social science.[1]

Cambridge social ontology is an unusual project, in terms of both its longevity and its focus on the importance of studying the nature of social reality. It has survived and had some significant impact, despite its resolute opposition to the hugely dominant mainstream of modern economics. Moreover, it has consistently highlighted the pressing need to prioritise ontological analysis in a disciplinary context where the legitimacy of such an agenda of research is rarely recognised. Given the state of mainstream academic economics, it is difficult to believe that a project like Cambridge social ontology has persisted and thrived. But it has. Therefore, before turning to social positioning theory, I aim, in this chapter, to examine the conditions that have allowed such a project to develop. I do so by exploring the institutional conditions and intellectual engagement with associated projects that have served to foster the development of Cambridge social ontology.

DOI: 10.4324/9781003110873-1

To start, I provide some background regarding the history of the Cambridge group, the meetings through which it has developed—the Cambridge Realist Workshop and the Cambridge Social Ontology Group—its approach to social ontology and the contributions of its members. I underline that, while this is a group project, the key figure, especially in relation to the development of social positioning theory, is Tony Lawson. I then consider two associated projects with which the Cambridge group has been linked. I begin by clarifying the relationship between Cambridge social ontology and critical realism and, in particular, the work of Roy Bhaskar. I then acknowledge the broader revival of scholarly interest in issues of social ontology and situate the Cambridge project in relation to these wider developments. In particular, I discuss the engagement between the Cambridge project and the project that developed along similar lines in Berkeley, most notably through the work of John Searle. Finally, I contextualise the more recent turn the group has made to focus specifically on developing social positioning theory.

The Cambridge Realist Workshop and the Cambridge Social Ontology Group

The beginnings of the Cambridge social ontology project can be traced back to research and initiatives instigated by Tony Lawson.[2] Some of Lawson's research in the early 1980s concerned a critique of the methods that dominated in economics and this provided the impetus for broader philosophical reflection regarding the nature of economics' object of study, social phenomena. It is, therefore, most accurate to describe Cambridge social ontology as beginning well over a decade before the start of the Cambridge Social Ontology Group, with Lawson meeting with students working with him to discuss issues that it would soon become clear were all related, in one way or another, to social ontology. As group member Stephen Pratten has explained:

> It all started in the late 1980s when a number of Cambridge research students, many of whom were working with Tony Lawson on methodological and philosophical issues relating to economics, began to meet up regularly to discuss topics of common interest. It became customary to meet on Monday evenings. Though informal at first, these Monday meetings eventually evolved into the *Cambridge Realist Workshop*. The first official meeting of the latter took place in October 1990.
> (Pratten, 2015c, p. 2)[3]

From an informal meeting between Lawson and his research students, the group first formalised its meetings not as the Cambridge Social Ontology Group but as the Cambridge Realist Workshop, which continues today.[4] If, at the beginning, the Cambridge Realist Workshop fostered the kind of open, regular, continuing discussion that characterises the Cambridge Social Ontology Group, its structure developed over time to involve speakers presenting papers, and, consequently, it became not only a far more formal occasion, but each week had its own distinct topic. Both the openness of discussion and the continuity in inquiry progressively decreased:

> When we started out the Realist Workshop it was a very informal, organically developing sort of endeavour. [. . .] After about ten years or so the Realist Workshop had changed. It was still meeting on Monday nights, but it was no longer this organic group we started with where we read each others' papers. Many of the original attendees had left Cambridge to gain academic employment. And the emphasis had become less personal. It had become more another type of performance. People come from around the world, famous people are coming in and give their talks, Nobel Memorial Prize winners like Amartya Sen or whoever. Each talk, though, is understandably usually unconnected with that of the previous week, and the audience can vary from week to week as well. It has remained a wonderful intellectual event. But en route we lost that organic character we had in the beginning. We lost the idea of developing our ideas together as a group.
>
> (Lawson, 2009, p. 120)

So, in October 2002, the Cambridge Social Ontology Group was founded with the aim of providing a forum to continue the sort of informal, ongoing discussion that fostered the early ontological inquiry pursued in Cambridge. The group, or CSOG (pronounced seesog) as it is more commonly known, has been meeting on Tuesday mornings ever since (Pratten, 2015c, p. 3).[5] The Cambridge Social Ontology Group is consequently a very different kind of meeting to the current Cambridge Realist Workshop. It is a smaller group. No papers are given. There are no pre-requisite readings. Research is conducted through discussion pursued in a largely unstructured manner. The only requirement is that members commit to attending regularly and are interested in taking part in the exploration of ontological issues. In Lawson's own words:

> What we do there is basically discuss topics in ontology. The structure is variable. A topic can last for an hour, or for a term and more. We spent about a term discussing the nature of gender, even longer discussing the nature of rules. We have even discussed the nature of econometrics. [. . .] [P]eople are expected to come to each meeting and the discussion progresses. [. . .] [W]e explore limitations of our shared beliefs. Sometimes it almost feels like a confessional. We question and re-question everything, not least the things we defend quite strongly in public. And we do laugh a lot. We continually criticise

ourselves. We also go round and round in dialectical circles, trying to make sure that everything is coherent with everything else, following every criticism and change in understanding—though we rarely succeed. No one feels the need to be protective about anything. Everyone's ego is left outside the room. It is very enjoyable and rewarding. The meetings are supposed to last two hours but usually they go on longer. When we are really keen or excited we fit in additional meetings at night times in pubs, or we may meet over vacations. As I say it is basically an ontology talk shop. But everyone involved seems to get a lot out of it.

(Lawson, 2009, pp. 120–121)

I have now been attending the Cambridge Social Ontology Group since 2016 and the above accurately describes my experience. Since I have been involved, discussions have focused on topics as varied as the nature of information, absences, meaning and time. There is an openness to discussing any and all topics but that is not to suggest that the group simply goes off untethered in all directions. I would also not wish to suggest that members of the group agree on everything. Far from it, debate is what makes Tuesday mornings interesting. Broadly speaking, and particularly in relation to the Cambridge social ontology project's original focus on issues in economics, the common threads have been characterised in the following way:

Although there is certainly no blanket consensus among participants in the Cambridge group, a good deal is shared at the level of philosophical objectives and broad evaluations. Most especially all participants hold to the view that the by-now-widely-recognised generalised explanatory failures and lack of realisticness of modern economics is directly related to pervasive ontological neglect. [. . .] This neglect and scientistic concern has rendered the widespread failings of modern economics almost inevitable. In any case, the approach of the Cambridge group has been different. Here the view accepted by all is that method and substantive theory can benefit if informed by explicit, systematic and sustained social ontology, and indeed that advances in method, substantive theory and ontology are best produced together with developments in each informing the others.

(Pratten, 2015c, p. 2)

While the above accurately describes a number of the shared concerns that have brought participants in the Cambridge social ontology project together, I would go further. Over time, concepts have developed to account, in general terms, for how social phenomena are constituted. While there may be disagreements over detail, and, indeed, these concepts are constantly evolving, I would suggest that underpinning the work of the Cambridge Social Ontology Group is a continually developing general social ontological conception. Perhaps this has not always been the case, but there are now more than just a set of shared concerns that characterise the discussions of the Cambridge Social Ontology Group. There is a shared, if evolving and debated, set of ontological concepts that aim to describe how social phenomena are everywhere constituted that can now be appropriately referred to as social positioning theory.[6]

Conceptions such as social positioning theory that apply generally to the constitution of social phenomena are the result of a form of study that Lawson distinguishes, under the umbrella of social ontology, as philosophical social ontology. Indeed, in Cambridge social ontology, differently from other conceptions of social ontology, a distinction is drawn between two related but different forms of social ontological inquiry, philosophical social ontology and scientific social ontology[7]:

> In my research I have found it useful to make a distinction between *socio-philosophical* ontology and *socio-scientific* ontology. The former is concerned with features that hold or operate *throughout* the social domain—that is, features of social being *per se*, that comprise in effect (or anyway include) basic principles according to which social reality is everywhere constituted. In contrast, socio-scientific ontology is concerned with how *particular* outcomes or social existents (money, markets, cities, corporations, technology, gender, universities) are formed, based on, or in line with, the more general features elaborated within philosophical ontology.
>
> (Lawson, 2019b, p. 11)

Philosophical social ontology focuses on elaborating features of social reality constitution that apply to social phenomena everywhere. Scientific social ontology, often drawing on the results of philosophical social ontological inquiry, studies the constitution of specific social phenomena such as those identified earlier. These forms of inquiry, while distinct, are linked not only through scientific social ontology drawing on philosophical social ontology but also through advances made in scientific social ontological inquiry coming to bear on the general philosophical social ontological conception. Indeed, much of the work of the Cambridge Social Ontology Group can be interpreted as a dialectical back and forth between philosophical social ontology and scientific social ontology. General concepts are used to inquire as to the nature of specific social existents and then results from studying such specific phenomena are in turn used to challenge and develop the general concepts employed and so on. This evolving conception of philosophical social ontology intertwined with projects in scientific social ontology ties the Cambridge social ontology project together.

This is a group endeavour. While some members have published more extensively than others, ideas are developed through continuing group interaction. And different members do take the lead in particular avenues of ontological inquiry. For example, members of the group have pursued projects in scientific social ontology focused on the natures of technology, the corporation and money.[8] On technology, advances have been made by C. Lawson (2017) and Faulkner and Runde (2013, 2019). On the corporation, there have been contributions by Deakin (2017); Lawson (2014a, 2015c, 2019b); Martins (2018a); Veldman and Willmott (2017). On money, a conception is developing with the work of Lawson (2016c, 2018a, 2018b, 2019a; 2019b, pp. 155–195; 2022a, 2022b) Peacock (2017) and through debate with Ingham (2018) and Searle (2017). Moreover, a substantial amount of research conducted by members of the Cambridge group has also been focused on the history of thought, particularly in economics. These include, for example, work by Lawson (2013, 2014b, 2015b); Lewis (2017, 2021); Lewis and Dold (2020); Lourenço and Graça Moura (2020); Martins (2014, 2019, 2020, 2021a, 2021b, 2023); Pratten (2015c, 2019, 2020, 2021) and Ragkousis (2023). Indeed, one key contribution has been to draw out the often implicit ontological presuppositions that are common to different schools of thought broadly categorised as belonging to heterodox economics (Lawson, 2006, 2013, 2021; Morgan, 2015; Slade-Caffarel, 2019).[9] In terms of social positioning theory, however, the results of philosophical social ontological inquiry have been overwhelmingly published by Lawson.[10] Therefore, as I explore the different features of social positioning theory, my focus, by and large, will be on Lawson's publications.

Above all, it is the conditions provided by the Cambridge Realist Workshop and, most importantly, the Cambridge Social Ontology Group that have fostered the continuing development of the Cambridge social ontology project. The group, however, does not operate in isolation and, over time, there has been important intellectual engagement with associated projects. Two such projects warrant particular consideration. I begin with Cambridge social ontology's engagement with critical realism and particularly the work of Roy Bhaskar. I then turn to the growing field of social ontology and, in particular, the conception developed by John Searle.

Critical realism

The research produced by members of the Cambridge Social Ontology Group has been closely associated with the project known as critical realism (Fleetwood, 1999; Lawson, 1997, 2003). Indeed, "[t]he contributions of the Cambridge group have often been referred to by its members and others under the title of critical realism in economics" (Pratten, 2015c, p. 10). However, this association has led to the Cambridge social ontology project sometimes being mistakenly interpreted as building upon the results of particular projects within critical realism and, in particular, the work of Roy Bhaskar. This is simply not the case. The relationship between the Cambridge group and critical realism is far more nuanced.

Rather, the development of a particular critique of economics by researchers associated with the Cambridge social ontology project grounded in a philosophical perspective appropriately characterised as realist had begun before an engagement with other similar projects in other disciplines, let alone with Bhaskar's work. The adoption of the label critical realism, at least for the Cambridge group, did not come about through building on the results of any particular critique—not even Bhaskar's. Rather, as a consequence of the fact that the Cambridge group's already developed concerns coincided with those of other projects, the adoption of a collective label seemed appropriate:

> At around the same time a series of similar related critiques of current social scientific practice in various different disciplines were being developed. Meanwhile Roy Bhaskar, partly drawing on the work of Rom Harré (1970) and Harré and Madden (1975), had recently developed a critique of the then dominant positions in the philosophy of science. These differently situated projects came together picking up especially on Bhaskar's philosophical language and formed a loose federation that placed a high priority on ontological analysis and elaboration and involved regular conferences and considerable interdisciplinary interaction. The label of critical realism was adopted by a number of these related but differently situated projects.
> (Pratten, 2015c, p. 10)

Developments made by Lawson and early participants in the Cambridge social ontology project coincided with those of other projects that found it useful to draw on the philosophical language developed by Bhaskar. Therefore, it made sense at that point in time to unite under a label, critical realism. But this was always a "loose federation". Over time, as these different projects developed, including Bhaskar's own, divergences emerged such that simply categorising contributions to the Cambridge social ontology project under the banner of critical realism could be misleading, especially if this was taken to mean that the results of analysis were entirely consistent with Bhaskar's work. Therefore, more recently, there has been a move towards identifying research associated with members of the Cambridge Social Ontology Group as being part of a distinct Cambridge social ontology project:

> [A]s the Cambridge project itself evolves, clarity is most likely to be served by elaborating precisely what it is that this project involves rather than establishing that the results achieved are entirely consistent with, still less emerge immediately from, a broader critical realist framework. Thus, although earlier papers make explicit reference to critical realism, sometimes even in the titles to contributions, and while there is no particular desire to distance the project from critical

realist contributions, for reasons of clarity it is currently more common for papers by Cambridge group participants to be presented simply as contributions to social ontology.

(Pratten, 2015c, pp. 10–11)

For Lawson, in particular, it is important to underline that while Bhaskar and other authors associated with the critical realist project have undoubtedly influenced his thinking, his development of a realist philosophical position predates engagement with those authors. Rather, Lawson's philosophical views developed early on through criticising the mainstream of economics as well as drawing on the work of economists, such as Keynes, to elaborate his philosophical arguments (Hendry, 1983; Kilpatrick & Lawson, 1980; Lawson, 1981, 1983, 1985, 1987, 1988).[11] Throughout that time, Lawson engaged with philosophy. Indeed, he "started researching philosophical issues around 1979 to 1980" (Dunn & Lawson, 2009, p. 485). At first, Lawson (2009, p. 102) "read anyone and everyone. I read quite a bit of Aristotle, Marx, Hegel, Kant, Hume, Whitehead—and many others. I also read people like Bas van Fraassen". But:

> [I]t wasn't until very late in the 1980s that I discovered the project called critical realism and Roy Bhaskar. [. . .] When I did come across Bhaskar's [. . .] book [*A Realist Theory of Science*] it mainly resonated. My copy of it contains a list of ticks. It was just so similar to some of the things I'd been saying myself, albeit in a different language. I think it was probably when I further realised that other social theorists in sociology and geography and elsewhere were beginning to adopt a lot of the philosophical terminology employed in critical realism, that I decided to do so too.
>
> (Dunn & Lawson, 2009, pp. 485–486)

To be accurate, then, Lawson's philosophical position began to develop before there was any engagement with critical realism. It coincided, at a time—and perhaps still, in parts, today—with much of the approach taken by Bhaskar as well as others such as Margaret Archer, Andrew Collier, Alan Norrie, Doug Porpora and Andrew Sayer.[12] This then led to coordination and the adoption of a common philosophical vocabulary. Even recently, Lawson (2019b, p. 10) "for a period of about six years [. . .] participated annually in a project on *social morphogenesis* directed by Margaret Archer".[13]

I do not wish to downplay the importance that engagement with critical realism has played in the development of the Cambridge social ontology project. However, although Lawson and the Cambridge group have at times presented their work as part of the critical realist project and have adopted a similar philosophical language, they have always pursued what was, and continues to be, a distinct project. For the reasons cited earlier, there has, therefore, in recent years, been a sustained movement in published contributions away from framing contributions made by members of the Cambridge group in terms of critical realism. Indeed, Lawson (2011, p. 59) has explained that "since the term ontology has, in recent years, become more commonplace [. . .] in social theory quite widely, I have been content to describe my basic project simply as one in social ontology". This has led some to question whether or not Lawson himself, or the Cambridge group more generally, still consider themselves to be critical realists. Lawson has responded to this question by stating:

> My project is characterised by a turn to ontology in social theory as an explicit undertaking. This is what I have been doing since the late 1970s. So I am actually very happy to be perceived as a critical realist. It is not at all a misinterpretation. But it is important to see this project as multifaceted and continuously evolving. And it is also variously interpreted.
>
> (Lawson, 2009, p. 103)

Moreover, most recently, Lawson has stated:

> I haven't changed in my commitment to Critical Realism as I all along understood it. However, I think the way that many now interpret or use the term Critical Realism is often at odds with my own under-standing. [. . .] So, I find it is simply less likely to mislead if on each occasion I spell out the assessments to which I commit, rather than relying on a label to speak for itself.
>
> (Lawson & Morgan, 2021, p. 77)

If there has been a shift insofar as contributions are less readily pre-sented as being about critical realism or critical realism in economics, the relationship between the Cambridge group and critical realism has not sub-stantially shifted. Cambridge social ontology has always been a distinct project that has shared concerns and philosophical language with other projects that have come under the banner of critical realism. That remains the case today. However, as the different projects that come under that ban-ner evolve, and so as not to suggest mistakenly that the results of the on-tological inquiry pursued by the Cambridge group are always consistent with the results of other such projects, the choice has been made to, more precisely, refer to the work produced by the group in terms of social ontol-ogy and, even more recently, as Cambridge social ontology specifically.

Searle and analytic social ontology

In recent years, there has been enormous growth in the amount of research presented under the banner of social ontology. This is in large part due to the substantial amount of work in social ontology that has emerged through building upon research conducted predominantly by analytic philosophers who study collective intentionality. Searle (2010, p. 10) wrote that "[c]ollective intentionality has recently become something of a cottage industry in analytic philosophy. There is even a biennial conference with the title 'Collective Intentionality'". Over time, the emphasis has moved from collective intentionality to social ontology and individuals associated with research relating to collective intentionality have founded both the International Social Ontology Society, in 2012, and the *Journal of Social Ontology*, in 2015.[14] Since 2018, the "Collective Intentionality" conference has been retitled "Social Ontology" and is held annually. Social ontology is growing in prominence within a school of thought that has historically been sceptical of ontology.[15]

Key contributions to this project have been made by authors such as Bratman (1999, 2007, 2014); Epstein (2015); Gilbert (1990, 1992, 1996, 2000, 2014); Guala (2016); Guala and Hindriks (2015); Ludwig (2016, 2017); Miller (2001, 2010); Schmid (2009); Searle (1995, 2010) and Tuomela (2002, 2007, 2013). And efforts have been made to define social ontology in terms of the concerns associated with such research (Epstein, 2018). However, while this output, within this emerging field, currently constitutes the dominant body of research in social ontology, there are a variety of approaches in social ontology.[16] This school—perhaps appropriately referred to as analytic social ontology—is one among many.[17] Within analytic social ontology, the most influential contribution has been made by John Searle.

If Lawson and the Cambridge group's engagement with this larger project has been limited, that is not the case when it comes to Searle and the Berkeley Social Ontology Group. Generally speaking, the work produced by the Cambridge group has not been engaged with in any sustained way by academic philosophers.[18] Moreover, Lawson has also had his own reasons for not engaging more generally with the mainstream of academic philosophy. But although there has been a resistance on behalf of many academic philosophers, that has not been the case with Searle:

> I do not have much contact with academic philosophers, less perhaps than I should. This is mainly because I find them, by and large, to be overly analytical, more concerned with being thought to be clever than with addressing matters about the way the world is, which is my interest. By and large I find the best philosophy, or anyway that which connects most with my own interests, is done outside philosophy departments. But John Searle is fundamentally interested in the way the world is [. . .]. Indeed, Searle's work on the constitution of society is ignored by many philosophers precisely because it is insufficiently like their conception of proper analytic philosophy. Searle's contributions, I think, like those of critical realism, are much more influential amongst natural and social scientists than amongst philosophers. Actually, I did take up an invitation to visit Searle and his ontology

group in Berkeley last summer, for about five weeks. In fact I went twice, because I was also earlier invited by Searle to give a talk at his bi-annual Collective Intentionality Conference, which [. . .] also featured Tuomela and Gilbert. It was a very fruitful experience for me. [. . .] I do not see a big conflict in our projects, certainly not between mine and Searle's. Searle actually thinks that we agree on just about everything. I am not so sure, but he well may be right. Certainly we agree on rather a lot.

(Lawson, 2009, p. 119)

Lawson's trips to Berkeley were followed by two workshops held in Cambridge, in 2014 and 2017, discussing critical issues in social ontology with members of the Berkeley Social Ontology Group:

[O]n two occasions over the last few years, participants of the Berkeley Social Ontology Group organised by Jennifer Hudin and John Searle visited Cambridge for joint workshops with the Cambridge group. Some of the interactions and related interventions have formed the content of papers that also have been published along the way.

(Lawson, 2019b, p. 10)

Most notably, these interactions have produced contributions from Lawson (2012, 2016b, 2016d, 2018b) and Searle (2016, 2017), in which they have debated and directly addressed each other's contributions. Consequently, much of Lawson's recent work has drawn very usefully on Searle's conception as a point of comparison and has benefitted from responding to critique from Searle himself. Indeed, following Lawson, I, in exploring social positioning theory, at times draw on Searle as a point of comparison where this serves to further enhance and clarify my analysis. This engagement with Searle has also encouraged Lawson to provide more detail regarding his conception of philosophical social ontology. But it is difficult to say the extent to which Searle's conception of social ontology has influenced Lawson's own.

One area in which there does seem to have been some influence is in how Lawson has presented his conception of social ontology. Lawson has at times characterised the process through which he has inquired as to the nature of the basic structure of social phenomena as working backwards in contrast to Searle, whose process he has described as working forwards:

[A] [. . .] relevant difference concerns the manner in which Searle and I have gone about our theorising, and in particular our contrasting starting points. The latter especially reflect the different priorities given to the constraint of ontological naturalism. My own approach is multifaceted, but a central component has been to proceed by first identifying generalised features of experience concerning (aspects of) human interactions and then to question whether any of their

preconditions (i.e. the conditions that must be in place for these ex-
perienced interactions and aspects to be possible) include those that
are additionally irreducible outcomes of human interactions (and if so
to explore their natures, etc.). If such human-interaction-dependent
features are so identified, then, being causally efficacious conditions
of (further) human interaction they can be accepted as real and being
products of human interaction they are seen additionally to be social.
The conception of social ontology I defend (and elaborate upon in due
course below) is to a significant extent a result of such endeavour. If
my approach might be appropriately described as *working backwards*
(from actual social interactions to their conditions of possibility),
Searle's alternative is perhaps best described as *working forwards*—
by way of building on the results of natural sciences regarded as the
most sound.

(Lawson, 2012, p. 347)[19]

I do not wish to enter into a discussion about the different processes
of philosophical inquiry pursued by Searle and Lawson, and I would not
venture to suggest that I have any idea what goes on in their minds. I am
sure that inquiry over several decades and, in both cases, involving much
group activity, has proceeded in a multitude of ways. However, the working backwards/working forwards distinction can be usefully employed to
distinguish between the different ways in which Lawson and Searle's respective conceptions have been set out. For regardless of how inquiry has
occurred, and whether or not Lawson still works backwards in his mind,
it is clear that in earlier work there was a substantial difference in the way
in which he presented his conception of philosophical social ontology on
paper. Lawson, previously, working backwards, would outline things in
the following way:

A [. . .] generalised feature of experience is that the practices people
follow, including routines (which may or may not become habitual),
are highly, and *systematically*, segmented or differentiated. It seems
we are not in all cases all empowered to do the same sorts of things.
Teachers follow routines and other recognisable practices which are
different to those followed by students. Similarly there are differences
between the regular practices of employers and those of employees,
between those of landladies/landlords and those of tenants, and so
forth. It is the case, then, that either we do not all follow the same
rules, or that given social rules lay down contrasting obligations, etc.,
for different (sorts of) people. How can this be? We can make sense of
all this by recognising that the constituents of social reality include *positions* into which people essentially slot, positions that have rules associated with them governing the obligations and perks, etc., that fall
on, or are on offer to, their occupants. This real category of positions

into which people slot is required to make sense of (is a necessary condition of the possibility of) the continuity of social life in the face of changing individuals; and it is the association of rules with these (different) positions that explains the systematic segmentation of routines followed.

(Lawson, 2003, pp. 38–39)

Here—with an early account of the existence of positions—Lawson starts with the generalised experience that, within the practices that we partake in, there is often a differentiation between individuals. The practices that individuals are able, and required, to take part in differ from individual to individual. Working backwards, Lawson argues that the condition of possibility for such differentiation is the existence of positions with associated differentiated rights and obligations—which he previously refers to as rules—that orient actions differently. Now regardless of how such ideas were conceived, there is a shift in more recent work towards presenting the account of philosophical social ontology in a manner more similar to Searle. Searle's accounts begin by setting out ontological features that apply generally to social and non-social phenomena, such as the laws of physics and evolutionary biology, and then showing how features specific to social phenomena are built upon such general ontological features and are able to account for the existence of social phenomena. Over the last decade, Lawson has begun accounts of philosophical social ontology in much the same way, starting with the common features of the constitution of both non-social and social phenomena before turning to those elements that render social phenomena distinct from other phenomena. In this way, the account makes abundantly clear that the conception presented is consistent with our best understanding of the nature of non-social phenomena.

I would not, however, want to exaggerate the extent to which the conception of social ontology defended in Cambridge has been influenced by Searle's own conception. Indeed, one would be mistaken to think that Lawson and Searle are always drawing on the same notions, even when a common vocabulary is involved (Slade-Caffarel, 2022). If the engagement between the Lawson and Cambridge Social Ontology Group and Searle and the Berkeley Social Ontology Group has undoubtedly positively contributed to the continuing development of Cambridge social ontology, much as with critical realism, although there may be some conceptual overlap, a clear set of common interests and very useful engagement, Cambridge social ontology remains its own distinct project.

Concluding remarks

The Cambridge social ontology project has been developing for the best part of the last four decades and the Cambridge Social Ontology Group has been meeting regularly for the last two decades. The project's survival is surprising, given a hostile institutional environment in which the modern mainstream of economics is overwhelmingly dominant. But Cambridge social ontology has fruitfully engaged with associated projects over its history, most notably critical realism and the growing field of social ontology—in particular, the work of John Searle.

In examining these influences, it is clear that, although there has been overlap and helpful engagement, Cambridge social ontology remains a distinct project with, at its core, weekly meetings—originally in the form of the Cambridge Realist Workshop and now, most importantly, with the Cambridge Social Ontology Group. These local institutional arrangements are the key to its longevity. Unlike other academic projects, the Cambridge Social Ontology Group has no pre-requisite readings; there is little formality, all that is required is an interest in discussing the nature of stuff. Over time, projects have developed and explanatorily powerful contributions have been produced. These are then constantly questioned and, at least for now, there is no sign of the group running out of things to talk about.

Over the last decade, there has been a renewed focus on philosophical social ontology which has resulted in the development of social positioning theory. If Lawson (1994, p. 521) has included a notion of positions since his very early work, he originally referred to internally related social positions as part of a "system of relational defined position-practices"[20] and for a long time, social positions were only recognised as being among the elements that make up social structure. For example, Lawson (2003, p. 39) presents positions as being but one part of social structure, explaining that "the constituents of social reality include positions into which people essentially slot".

A focus on social positioning as *the* central category came later. Indeed, social positioning only really began to take prominence within the developing conception of social ontology as part of two projects in scientific social ontology. It is in elaborating conceptions of the nature of the corporation and of money that Lawson seems to have recognised the explanatory power associated with the notion of social positioning and, consequently, its key role in the constitution of social phenomena everywhere (Lawson, 2014a, 2015c, 2016c, 2018a, 2018b, 2019b). From that point onwards, Lawson has consistently stated that social phenomena are everywhere constituted through processes of social positioning:

> All social phenomena that we identify are constituted through processes of social positioning (a feature that goes unnoticed in most social theorising).
>
> (Lawson, 2014a, p. 3)

> Social positioning is an essential and central feature in the production and reproduction of social reality.
>
> (Lawson, 2016a, p. 249)

[P]rocesses of social positioning are central to the constitution of all of social reality.

(Lawson, 2016c, p. 962)

[E]verything social is constituted via (or in relation to) processes of social positioning [. . .].

(Lawson, 2016c, p. 963)

[S]ocial reality everywhere is constituted via processes of social positioning.

(Lawson, 2019b, p. 155)

At the heart of the theory of social positioning is the thesis that novel social phenomena are everywhere constituted by or within processes through which social totalities (human communities, artefacts, language and communication systems, etc.) are formed or emerge. Through these processes various, mostly pre-existing, elements are relationally organised in ways whereby they are formed into components of the emergent totalities. It is the *organisation* of these elements that is key to social constitution. And according to social positioning theory, all forms of social organisation depend on processes of social positioning.

(Lawson, 2022a, p. 1)

Social positioning theory accounts for this assessment. I turn now to detailing its features.

Notes

1 For more on Lawson's critique of the modern mainstream of economics, see, for example, Fullbrook (2009); Lawson (1997, 2003, 2006, 2013, 2015b, 2021); Martins (2014); Morgan (2015); Pratten (2007, 2015c) and Slade-Caffarel (2019).
2 Faulkner, Pratten, and Runde (2017, p. 1265) note that the "central figure in this project is Tony Lawson, whose work has provided much of the impetus for Cambridge Social Ontology over the last thirty years".
3 Pratten also provides an extract from the open letter sent by Tony Lawson on 15 October 1990 in advance of the first meeting:

> Although it is anticipated that the workshop will entail some philosophical (as well as History of Thought) orientation, the concern is centrally with the doing of substantive economics. All that is presupposed is a commitment to the view that there exists a knowable (under some description) social reality and that economics should primarily address such matters as identifying and understanding real world economic structures, mechanisms, processes and events, etc. This commitment, though minimal, does entail acknowledging that the nature of economic reality bears upon both the types of theories we can legitimately entertain as well as the methods of theory assessment that can be rationally supported. In philosophical

jargon it is a presupposition of the realist programme that questions of ontology are in some sense prior to, and bear upon, questions of epistemology and methodology as well as substantive economic research.

(Pratten, 2015c, pp. 2–3)

This letter interestingly underlines the focus on economics that has characterised much of the research output related to Cambridge social ontology. However, it also foreshadows the extent to which the key to it all is ontology.

4　Due to the COVID-19 pandemic, the Cambridge Realist Workshop went on hiatus in March of 2020. Meetings resumed online in October 2022.

5　The group met in the coffee room on the top floor of the Economics Faculty at the University of Cambridge until March of 2020 when, due to the COVID-19 pandemic, the group shifted its meetings online. Meetings continue on Tuesday mornings online to this day.

6　I acknowledge that Rom Harré has developed a positioning theory that has ostensible similarities to Lawson's and the Cambridge group's theory, such as the emphasis on positions, rights and, in Harré's terminology, duties. However, over and above the fact that Harré's positioning theory is not attempting to provide a conception of philosophical social ontology, with closer examination, one can identify important differences particularly in relation to how positions are conceived. For example, Harré (2012, p. 193) writes that "[a] cluster of short-term disputable rights, obligations, and duties is called a 'position'", which is very different to Lawson's conception. And that is before examining the role of features such as storylines in Harré's theory. Moreover, as far as I am aware, Harré's notion of positioning has had no influence on Lawson. For more on Harré's positioning theory, see Davies and Harré (1990); Harré (2012, 2015); Harré and Lagenhove (1999) and Harré and Moghaddam (2003).

7　This distinction draws on that made by Roy Bhaskar between scientific ontology and philosophical ontology:

Whenever there is any danger of confusion between an "ontology" in the sense of the kind of world presupposed by a philosophical account of science and in the sense of the particular entities and processes postulated by some substantive scientific theory I shall explicitly distinguish between a philosophical and a scientific ontology.

(Bhaskar, 2008 [1975], p. 19)

8　For an overview of the different projects in scientific social ontology dating back to the beginnings of the Cambridge Social Ontology project, see Pratten (2015a).

9　Work by members of the group is by no means limited to kind of research discussed earlier. Bacevic (2021), for example, has developed a notion of epistemic positioning. Meyenburg and Turcitu (2021) have discussed how vagueness may relate to social ontological theorising. Heuer and Runde (2021) have explored how social positioning theory can be used to understand how a building relates to the city in which it is located.

10　That is not to suggest that the group has not been involved in the development of social positioning theory. Recent contributions made by members other than Lawson to aspects of the conception of philosophical social ontology as well as social positioning theory specifically include Martins (2011, 2018b, 2022) and Pratten (2013, 2015b, 2017, 2020, 2023). For more on earlier stages in the development of the account of philosophical social ontology associated with the Cambridge Social Ontology project, see Fullbrook (2009); C. Lawson, Latsis, and Martins (2007) and Lawson (1997, 2003).

11 Lawson has written:

> I was based in Cambridge and Keynes was still something of a hero there, and the advantage of this situation for me was that if I took up an issue, laid down an argument or said something I wanted to say in the context of engaging with something Keynes had argued, my own topic was thereby considered legitimate. This was important in an academic discipline that tended to neglect, if not actively dismiss, methodological discussion. Martin Hollis somewhere accuses me of 'hitching a ride with Keynes,' and he wasn't completely wrong.
>
> (Dunn & Lawson, 2009, p. 486)

12 For an overview of these varied contributions, see Archer, Bhaskar, Collier, Lawson, and Norrie (1998).

13 See Archer (2013, 2014, 2015, 2016, 2017).

14 For more on the International Social Ontology Society, see https://isosonline. org. For more on the *Journal of Social Ontology*, see www.degruyter.com/view/j/ jso and Schmid et al. (2015). For an overview of engagement that such authors have had specifically with Searle's conception, see Tsohatzidis (2007).

15 As Latsis explains:

> Ontology, normally understood, is the science of being, the systematic study of the fundamental structure of reality. [Analytic] [p]hilosophers of the early twentieth century had distanced themselves from any ability to partake in such an activity. So discussions of ontology were both uncommon and unfashionable [. . .]. The logical positivists and empiricists who dominated analytic philosophy tended to regard it as obscure and outdated and references to ontology or metaphysics were usually pejorative.
>
> (Latsis, 2007, p. 128)

Interestingly, Searle writes:

> It is an odd fact of intellectual history that the great philosophers of the past century had little or nothing to say about social ontology. I am thinking of such figures as Frege, Russell, and Wittgenstein, as well as Quine, Carnap, Strawson, and Austin. But if they did not address the problems that interest me in this book, they did develop techniques of analysis and approaches to language that I intend to use.
>
> (Searle, 2010, p. 6)

Searle makes clear that while the major figures in analytic philosophy paid little to no interest to social ontology, which one could argue was in part due to their focus on a particular set of methods, he employs the same methods in his pursuit of social ontology.

16 I do not want to suggest, at all, that the only current prominent project in social ontology other than the Cambridge account is that which has emerged out of this project in collective intentionality. Work in social ontology is being done from other perspectives by authors such as Ásta (2018); Elder-Vass (2012); Groff (2013); Haslanger (2012); Ikaheimo and Laitinen (2011); Porpora (1987); Testa (2016) and Witt (2011).

17 Moreover, one could argue that analytic social ontology is quite late to the game. Although rarely presented as work in social ontology, the general disinterest in the study of being and, in particular, social being did not seemingly extend to authors associated, for lack of a better term, with continental philosophy. Indeed, major twentieth-century contributions by authors such as Jean-Paul Sartre and Michel Foucault, as well as authors associated with the Frankfurt School such as Theodor W. Adorno and Max Horkheimer have been interpreted as

contributions to social ontology. See, for example, Al-Amoudi (2007); de Warren (2016); de Warren (2017); Testa (2015).

18 This lack of engagement is, I suspect, for a variety of reasons. But I would suggest that perhaps the situation broadly mirrors the response the group's contributions have received on behalf of mainstream economists. Both fields, interestingly, have an overwhelmingly dominant mainstream that is largely un-interested in contributions that do not follow a particular set of methodological principles. One notable recent exception is Witt (2023).

19 The process Lawson refers to earlier as "working backwards" is that which he has alternatively referred to elsewhere as "transcendental argument", "transcendental analysis" and "transcendental reasoning". Previously, Law-son strongly emphasised the role that this approach played in developing an account of philosophical social ontology. Lawson (2003, p. 44) writes that "[i]t is clear, then, that we are able to make sense of various generalised features of certain human practices, by transcendentally deducing their conditions of possibility. In so doing we are led to a definite conception of social reality". For more, see Lawson (2003, pp. 28–63).

In recent years, however, Lawson has less commonly used terms such as transcendental argument and, when he has referred to his approach to doing social ontology, has done so in terms of the metaphor of "working backwards". A notable exception is Lawson (2015a), in which he not only discusses transcen-dental reasoning but also provides it as an explanation for why the study of philosophical social ontology is possible:

> The contention to be defended here, then, is that philosophical ontology need not be dogmatic and transcendent, but rather can be conditional and immanent. Quine allows that the theories of natural science constitute a le-gitimate entry point for scientific ontology just because, or where, they are taken as reliable. Reliability of entry points is the key here. But in seeking such reliability we are *not* constrained to consider, with Quine, only those claims that express the content of theories. It is just as legitimate, for ex-ample, to commence from any feature of experience regarded as adequate or successful to the relevant domain of reality, including most especially those concerning *human practices*. Of course, once this is recognised, it can be seen that ontology need not be restricted either to scientific (as opposed to philosophical) ontology or indeed to the study of non-social phenom-ena. Philosophical ontology, at least as conceived here, aims at generalised insights, and reliable conceptions of human practices and so forth can be sought that are also reasonably generalised, including those relating to successful natural scientific practices as well as to everyday social ones.
>
> (Lawson, 2015a, pp. 27–28)

Lawson goes on to say:

> [W]e can accept transcendental reasoning just as fallible, practically conditioned, investigation into some or other feature of our experience, a practice which in philosophical ontology takes the form of an investi-gation into generalised features of our experience, including of human practices. [. . .] There is no suggestion [. . .] that transcendental reasoning is the only method of philosophical ontology; no presumption that philo-sophical ontology is somehow restricted to that method. However, this consideration of the workings of transcendental argument does serve to indicate that philosophical ontology can be (and of course the argument here is that it must be) conditional and immanent.
>
> (Lawson, 2015a, p. 29)

Transcendental argument, then, has at times been a key component of how Lawson conceives of philosophical social ontology. However, it is unclear as to the role that transcendental argument plays currently in how Lawson conceives of his conception of philosophical social ontology and how it has been derived.
20 In greater detail, Lawson writes:

> [T]wo objects are said to be internally related if they are what they are by virtue of the relationship in which they stand to the other. Landlord and tenant, employer and employee, hunter and prey, magnet and its field are examples that spring easily to mind. In each case you cannot have the one without the other, each, in part, is what it is, and does what it does, by virtue of the relation in which it stands to the other. Of particular relevance here are the internal relations that hold between social *positions*. If it is the case, say, that presidents exercise different rights, obligations, tasks, duties, powers and so on, to the rest of us, or that, say, teachers exercise different rights and obligations to students, it is equally the case that the relevant rights, tasks, powers and so on exist independently of the particular individuals fulfilling these roles. At issue then is a system of relational defined position-practices, a system of positions, with associated practices, obligations and powers defined in relation to other such positions, and into which agents essentially slot. With reflection it should be clear that all social structures and systems—the economy, the state, international organisations, trade unions, and households, and the like—depend upon or presuppose social relations of this form. It is the position-practice system, then, and specifically the concept of a position into which individuals slot, that provides the concept of the contact point between agency and social structure.
>
> (Lawson, 1994, p. 521)

This terminology is consistent with that employed by Roy Bhaskar:

> [I]t is evident that we need a system of mediating concepts, encompassing both aspects of the duality of praxis, designating the "slots", as it were, in the social structure into which active subjects must slip in order to reproduce it; that is, a system of concepts designating the "point of contact" between human agency and social structures. Such a point, linking action to structure, must *both* endure and be immediately occupied by individuals. It is clear that the mediating system we need is that of the *positions* (places, functions, rules, tasks, duties, rights, etc.) occupied (filled, assumed, enacted, etc.) by individuals, and of the *practices* (activities, etc.) in which, in virtue of their occupancy of these positions (and vice versa), they engage. I shall call this mediating system the position-practice system.
>
> (Bhaskar, 2015 [1979], p. 44)

References

Al-Amoudi, I. (2007). Redrawing Foucault's social ontology. *Organization, 14*(4), 543–563. doi:10.1177/1350508407078052

Archer, M. S. (Ed.) (2013). *Social morphogenesis*. Dordrecht: Springer.

Archer, M. S. (Ed.) (2014). *Late modernity: Trajectories towards morphogenic society.* Dordrecht: Springer.

Archer, M. S. (Ed.) (2015). *Generative mechanisms transforming the social order.* Dordrecht: Springer.

Archer, M. S. (Ed.) (2016). *Morphogenesis and the crisis of normativity.* Dordrecht: Springer.

Archer, M. S. (Ed.) (2017). *Morphogenesis and human flourishing*. Dordrecht: Springer.

Archer, M. S., Bhaskar, R., Collier, A., Lawson, T., & Norrie, A. (Eds.). (1998). *Critical realism: Essential readings*. London and New York: Routledge.

Bacevic, J. (2021). Epistemic injustice and epistemic positioning: Towards an intersectional political economy. *Current Sociology, 71*(6), 1122–1140. doi:10.1177/00113921211057609

Bhaskar, R. (2008 [1975]). *A realist theory of science*. London and New York: Routledge.

Bhaskar, R. (2015 [1979]). *The possibility of naturalism: A philosophical critique of the contemporary human sciences* (Fourth edition. ed.). London and New York: Routledge.

Bratman, M. (1999). *Faces of intention: Selected essays on intention and agency*. Cambridge: Cambridge University Press.

Bratman, M. (2007). *Structures of agency: Essays*. Oxford: Oxford University Press.

Bratman, M. (2014). *Shared agency: A planning theory of acting together*. Oxford: Oxford University Press.

Davies, B., & Harré, R. (1990). Positioning: The discursive production of selves. *Journal for the Theory of Social Behaviour, 20*(1), 43–63. doi:10.1111/j.1468–5914.1990.tb00174.x

Deakin, S. (2017). Tony Lawson's theory of the corporation: Towards a social ontology of law. *Cambridge Journal of Economics, 41*(5), 1505–1523. doi:10.1093/cje/bex044

de Warren, N. (2016). Brothers in arms: Fraternity-terror in Sartre's social ontology. In T. Szanto & D. Moran (Eds.), *Phenomenology of sociality: Discovering the "we"* (pp. 313–327). New York: Taylor and Francis.

de Warren, N. (2017). We are, therefore I am-I am, therefore we are: The third in Sartre's social ontology. In C. Durt, T. Fuchs, & C. Tewes (Eds.), *Embodiment, enaction, and culture: Investigating the constitution of the shared world* (pp. 47–65). Cambridge: MIT Press.

Dunn, S. P., & Lawson, T. (2009). Cambridge economics, heterodoxy and ontology: An interview with Tony Lawson. *Review of Political Economy, 21*(3), 481–496. doi:10.1080/09538250902834095

Elder-Vass, D. (2012). *The reality of social construction*. Cambridge: Cambridge University Press.

Epstein, B. (2015). *The ant trap: Rebuilding the foundations of the social sciences*. Oxford: Oxford University Press.

Epstein, B. (2018). Social ontology. In E. N. Zalta (Ed.), *The Stanford encyclopedia of philosophy*. Stanford: Metaphysics Research Lab, Stanford University.

Faulkner, P., Pratten, S., & Runde, J. (2017). Cambridge social ontology: Clarification, development and deployment. *Cambridge Journal of Economics, 41*(5), 1265–1277. doi:10.1093/cje/bex048

Faulkner, P., & Runde, J. (2013). Technological objects, social positions, and the transformational model of social activity. *MIS Quarterly, 37*(3), 803–818. Retrieved from www.jstor.org/stable/43826001

Faulkner, P., & Runde, J. (2019). Theorizing the digital object. *MIS Quarterly, 43*(4), 1279–1302. doi:10.25300/MISQ/2019/13136

Fleetwood, S. (1999). *Critical realism in economics: Development and debate*. London and New York: Routledge.

Fullbrook, E. (Ed.) (2009). *Ontology and economics: Tony Lawson and his critics*. London and New York: Routledge.

Gilbert, M. (1990). Walking together: A paradigmatic social phenomenon. *Midwest Studies in Philosophy, 15*(1), 1–14. doi:10.1111/j.1475–4975.1990.tb00202.x

Gilbert, M. (1992). *On social facts*. Princeton, NJ: Princeton University Press.

Gilbert, M. (1996). *Living together: Rationality, sociality, and obligation*. Lanham, MD: Rowman & Littlefield Publishers.

Gilbert, M. (2000). *Sociality and responsibility: New essays in plural subject theory*. Lanham, MD: Rowman & Littlefield Publishers.

Gilbert, M. (2014). *Joint commitment: How we make the social world.* Oxford: Oxford University Press.

Groff, R. (2013). *Ontology revisited: Metaphysics in social and political philosophy.* London and New York: Routledge.

Guala, F. (2016). *Understanding institutions: The science and philosophy of living together.* Princeton, NJ: Princeton University Press.

Guala, F., & Hindriks, F. (2015). A unified social ontology. *The Philosophical Quarterly, 65*(259), 177–201. doi:10.1093/pq/pqu072

Harré, R. (1970). *The principles of scientific thinking.* Chicago: University of Chicago Press.

Harré, R. (2012). Positioning theory: Moral dimensions of social-cultural psychology. In J. Valsiner (Ed.), *The Oxford handbook of culture and psychology* (pp. 191–207). Oxford: Oxford University Press.

Harré, R. (2015). Positioning theory. In J. Martin, J. Sugarman, & K. L. Slaney (Eds.), *The Wiley handbook of theoretical and philosophical psychology: Methods, approaches, and new directions for social sciences* (pp. 263–277). Chichester, West Sussex: Wiley Blackwell.

Harré, R., & Lagenhove, L. V. (1999). *Positioning theory: Moral contexts of intentional action.* Oxford: Blackwell.

Harré, R., & Madden, E. (1975). *Causal powers.* Oxford: Blackwell.

Harré, R., & Moghaddam, F. M. (2003). *The self and others: Positioning individuals and groups in personal, political, and cultural contexts.* Westport, CT: Praeger.

Haslanger, S. (2012). *Resisting reality: Social construction and social critique.* Oxford: Oxford University Press.

Hendry, D. F. (1983). On Keynesian model building and the rational expectations critique: A question of methodology. *Cambridge Journal of Economics, 7*(1), 69–75. doi:10.1093/oxfordjournals.cje.a035527

Heuer, T., & Runde, J. (2021). The Elbphilharmonie and the Hamburg effect: On the social positioning, identities and system functions of a building and a city. *European Planning Studies, 30*(1), 85–104. doi:10.1080/09654313.2021.1908232

Ikaheimo, H., & Laitinen, A. (Eds.). (2011). *Recognition and social ontology.* Leiden: Brill.

Ingham, G. (2018). A critique of Lawson's "Social positioning and the nature of money". *Cambridge Journal of Economics, 42*(3), 837–850. doi:10.1093/cje/bex070

Kilpatrick, A., & Lawson, T. (1980). On the nature of industrial decline in the UK. *Cambridge Journal of Economics, 4*(1), 85–102. doi:10.1093/oxfordjournals.cje.a035441

Latsis, J. (2007). Quine and the ontological turn in economics. In C. Lawson, J. Latsis, & N. Martins (Eds.), *Contributions to social ontology* (pp. 127–141). London and New York: Routledge.

Lawson, C. (2017). *Technology and isolation.* Cambridge: Cambridge University Press.

Lawson, C., Latsis, J., & Martins, N. (Eds.). (2007). *Contributions to social ontology.* London and New York: Routledge.

Lawson, T. (1981). Keynesian model building and the rational expectations critique. *Cambridge Journal of Economics, 5*(4), 311–326. doi:10.1093/oxfordjournals.cje.a035489

Lawson, T. (1983). Different approaches to economic modelling. *Cambridge Journal of Economics, 7*(1), 77–84. doi:10.1093/oxfordjournals.cje.a035528

Lawson, T. (1985). Uncertainty and economic analysis. *The Economic Journal, 95*(380), 909–927. doi:10.2307/2233256

Lawson, T. (1987). The relative/absolute nature of knowledge and economic analysis. *The Economic Journal, 97*, 951–970.

Lawson, T. (1988). Probability and uncertainty in economic analysis. *Journal of Post Keynesian Economics, 11*(1), 38–65. Retrieved from www.jstor.org/stable/4538115

Lawson, T. (1994). The nature of Post Keynesianism and its links to other traditions: A realist perspective. *Journal of Post Keynesian Economics, 16*(4), 503–538.

Lawson, T. (1997). *Economics and reality*. London and New York: Routledge.

Lawson, T. (2003). *Reorienting economics*. London and New York: Routledge.

Lawson, T. (2006). The nature of heterodox economics. *Cambridge Journal of Economics*, 30(4), 483–505.

Lawson, T. (2009). Cambridge social ontology: An interview with Tony Lawson. *Erasmus Journal for Philosophy and Economics*, 2(1), 100–122. doi:10.23941/ejpe. v2i1.26

Lawson, T. (2011). Anti-realism or pro-something else? Response to Deischel. *Erasmus Journal for Philosophy and Economics*, 4(1), 53–66.

Lawson, T. (2012). Ontology and the study of social reality: Emergence, organisation, community, power, social relations, corporations, artefacts and money. *Cambridge Journal of Economics*, 36(2), 345–385. doi:10.1093/cje/ber050

Lawson, T. (2013). What is this "school" called neoclassical economics. *Cambridge Journal of Economics*, 37(5), 947–983.

Lawson, T. (2014a). The nature of the firm and peculiarities of the corporation. *Cambridge Journal of Economics*, 39(1), 1–32. doi:10.1093/cje/beu046

Lawson, T. (2014b). Process, order and stability in Veblen. *Cambridge Journal of Economics*, 39(4), 993–1030. doi:10.1093/cje/beu045

Lawson, T. (2015a). A conception of social ontology. In S. Pratten (Ed.), *Social ontology and modern economics* (pp. 19–52). London and New York: Routledge.

Lawson, T. (2015b). *Essays on the nature and state of modern economics*. London and New York: Routledge.

Lawson, T. (2015c). The modern corporation: The site of a mechanism (of global social change) that is out-of-control? In M. S. Archer (Ed.), *Generative mechanisms transforming the social order* (pp. 205–231). Dordrecht: Springer.

Lawson, T. (2016a). Collective practices and norms. In M. S. Archer (Ed.), *Morphogenesis and the crisis of normativity* (pp. 249–279). Dordrecht: Springer.

Lawson, T. (2016b). Comparing conceptions of social ontology: Emergent social entities and/or institutional facts? *Journal for the Theory of Social Behaviour*, 46(4), 359–399. doi:10.1111/jtsb.12126

Lawson, T. (2016c). Social positioning and the nature of money. *Cambridge Journal of Economics*, 40(4), 961–996. doi:10.1093/cje/bew006

Lawson, T. (2016d). Some critical issues in social ontology: Reply to John Searle. *Journal for the Theory of Social Behaviour*, 46(4), 426–437.

Lawson, T. (2018a). The constitution and nature of money. *Cambridge Journal of Economics*, 42(3), 851–873. doi:10.1093/cje/bey005

Lawson, T. (2018b). Debt as money. *Cambridge Journal of Economics*, 42(4), 1165–1181. doi:10.1093/cje/bey006

Lawson, T. (2019a). Money's relation to debt: Some problems with MMT's conception of money. *Real-World Economics Review*(89), 109–128.

Lawson, T. (2019b). *The nature of social reality: Issues in social ontology*. London and New York: Routledge.

Lawson, T. (2021). Whatever happened to neoclassical economics? *Revue de philosophie économique*, 22(1), 39–84. doi:10.3917/rpec.221.0039

Lawson, T. (2022a). Social positioning theory. *Cambridge Journal of Economics*, 46(1), 1–39. doi:10.1093/cje/beab040

Lawson, T. (2022b). Two conceptions of the nature of money: Clarifying differences between MMT and money theories sponsored by social positioning theory. *Real-World Economics Review*, (101), 2–19.

Lawson, T., & Morgan, J. (2021). Cambridge social ontology, the philosophical critique of modern economics and social positioning theory: An interview with Tony Lawson, part 1. *Journal of Critical Realism*, 20(1), 72–97. doi:10.1080/14767430.2020.1846009

Lewis, P. (2017). Ontology and the history of economic thought: The case of anti-reductionism in the work of Friedrich Hayek. *Cambridge Journal of Economics*, 41(5), 1343–1365. doi:10.1093/cje/bex031

Lewis, P. (2021). Elinor's Ostrom's "realist orientation": An investigation of the ontological commitments of her analysis of the possibility of self-governance. *Journal of Economic Behavior & Organization, 189,* 623–636. doi:https://doi.org/10.1016/j.jebo.2021.07.021

Lewis, P., & Dold, M. (2020). James Buchanan on the nature of choice: Ontology, artifactual man and the constitutional moment in political economy. *Cambridge Journal of Economics, 44*(5), 1159–1179. doi:10.1093/cje/beaa027

Lourenço, D., & Graça Moura, M. (2020). Tony Lawson and the history of economic thought. *Cambridge Journal of Economics, 44*(5), 991–1011. doi:10.1093/cje/beaa030

Ludwig, K. (2016). *From individual to plural agency* (Vol. Volume 1). Oxford: Oxford University Press.

Ludwig, K. (2017). *From plural to institutional agency* (Vol. Volume 2). Oxford: Oxford University Press.

Martins, N. O. (2011). An evolutionary approach to emergence and social causation. *Journal of Critical Realism, 10*(2), 192–218. doi:10.1558/jcr.v10i2.192

Martins, N. O. (2014). *The Cambridge revival of political economy.* London and New York: Routledge.

Martins, N. O. (2018a). Justice and the social ontology of the corporation. *Journal of Business Ethics, 153*(1), 17–28. doi:10.1007/s10551–016–3360-y

Martins, N. O. (2018b). An ontology of power and leadership. *Journal for the Theory of Social Behaviour, 48*(1), 83–97. doi:10.1111/jtsb.12155

Martins, N. O. (2019). The Sraffian methodenstreit and the revolution in economic theory. *Cambridge Journal of Economics, 43*(2), 507–525. doi:10.1093/cje/bey059

Martins, N. O. (2020). Reconsidering the notions of process, order and stability in Veblen. *Cambridge Journal of Economics, 44*(5), 1115–1135. doi:10.1093/cje/beaa005

Martins, N. O. (2021a). The Cambridge economic tradition and the distribution of the social surplus. *Cambridge Journal of Economics, 45*(2), 225–241. doi:10.1093/cje/beaa049

Martins, N. O. (2021b). Development and the revival of political economy. *Journal of Economic Issues, 55*(1), 162–177. doi:10.1080/00213624.2021.1874797

Martins, N. O. (2022). Social positioning and the pursuit of power. *Cambridge Journal of Economics, 46*(2), 275–292. doi:10.1093/cje/beab057

Martins, N. O. (2023). Joan Robinson and the reconstruction of economic theory. *Cambridge Journal of Economics.* doi:10.1093/cje/bead018

Meyenburg, I., & Turcitu, A. M. (2021). Vagueness and social ontology: Implications of inquiry resistant borderline cases for social ontological theorising. *Journal for the Theory of Social Behaviour.* doi:10.1111/jtsb.12314

Miller, S. (2001). *Social action: A teleological account.* Cambridge: Cambridge University Press.

Miller, S. (2010). *The moral foundations of social institutions: A philosophical study.* Cambridge: Cambridge University Press.

Morgan, J. (2015). *What is neoclassical economics?: Debating the origins, meaning and significance.* London and New York: Routledge.

Peacock, M. S. (2017). The ontology of money. *Cambridge Journal of Economics, 41*(5), 1471–1487. doi:10.1093/cje/bex012

Porpora, D. V. (1987). *The concept of social structure.* New York: Greenwood Press.

Pratten, S. (2007). Ontological theorising and the assumptions issue in economics. In C. Lawson, J. Latsis, & N. Martins (Eds.), *Contributions to social ontology* (pp. 50–67). London and New York: Routledge.

Pratten, S. (2013). Critical realism and the process account of emergence. *Journal for the Theory of Social Behaviour, 43*(3), 251–279. doi:doi:10.1111/jtsb.12017

Pratten, S. (2015a). Introduction. In S. Pratten (Ed.), *Social ontology and modern economics* (pp. 1–16). London and New York: Routledge.

Pratten, S. (2015b). The scope of ontological theorising. In S. Pratten (Ed.), *Social ontology and modern economics* (pp. 68–94). London and New York: Routledge.

Pratten, S. (2015c). *Social ontology and modern economics*. London and New York: Routledge.

Pratten, S. (2017). Trust and the social positioning process. *Cambridge Journal of Economics, 41*(5), 1419–1436. doi:10.1093/cje/bex040

Pratten, S. (2019). Dewey on organisation. *European Journal of Pragmatism and American Philosophy, XI*(2). doi:10.4000/ejpap.1671

Pratten, S. (2020). Social positioning and Commons's monetary theorising. *Cambridge Journal of Economics, 44*(5), 1137–1157. doi:10.1093/cje/beaa036

Pratten, S. (2021). Veblen, Marshall and neoclassical economics. *Journal of Classical Sociology, 23*(1), 63–88. doi:10.1177/1468795x211068999

Pratten, S. (2023). The concept of function in social positioning theory. *Journal for the Theory of Social Behaviour, 53*(4), 560–582. doi:https://doi.org/10.1111/jtsb.12389

Ragkousis, A. (2024). Amartya Sen as a neoclassical economist. *Journal of Economic Issues, 58*(1), 24–58. doi:10.1080/00213624.2024.2307785

Schmid, H. B. (2009). *Plural action: Essays in philosophy and social science*. Dordrecht: Springer.

Schmid, H. B., Hindriks, F., Ikäheimo, H., Laitinen, A., Salice, A., & Schweikard David, P. (2015). Editorial note. In *Journal of Social Ontology* (Vol. 1, pp. v).

Searle, J. R. (1995). *The construction of social reality*. London: Penguin.

Searle, J. R. (2010). *Making the social world: The structure of human civilization*. Oxford: Oxford University Press.

Searle, J. R. (2016). The limits of emergence: Reply to Tony Lawson. *Journal for the Theory of Social Behaviour, 46*(6), 400–412. doi:10.1111/jtsb.12125

Searle, J. R. (2017). Money: Ontology and deception. *Cambridge Journal of Economics, 41*(5), 1453–1470. doi:10.1093/cje/bex034

Slade-Caffarel, Y. (2019). The nature of heterodox economics revisited. *Cambridge Journal of Economics, 43*(4), 527–539. doi:10.1093/cje/bey043

Slade-Caffarel, Y. (2022). Rights and obligations in Cambridge social ontology. *Journal for the Theory of Social Behaviour, 52*(2), 392–410. doi:10.1111/jtsb.12332

Ásta. (2018). *Categories we live by: The construction of sex, gender, race, and other social categories*. Oxford: Oxford University Press.

Testa, I. (2015). Ontology of the False State. *Journal of Social Ontology, 1*(2), 271–300. doi:10.1515/jso-2014-0025

Testa, I. (2016). Dewey's social ontology: A pragmatist alternative to Searle's approach to social reality. *International Journal of Philosophical Studies, 25*(1), 40–62. doi:10.1080/09672559.2016.1260625

Tsohatzidis, S. L. (2007). *Intentional acts and institutional facts: Essays on John Searle's social ontology*. Dordrecht: Springer.

Tuomela, R. (2002). *The philosophy of social practices: A collective acceptance view*. Cambridge: Cambridge University Press.

Tuomela, R. (2007). *The philosophy of sociality: The shared point of view*. Oxford England; New York: Oxford University Press.

Tuomela, R. (2013). *Social ontology: Collective intentionality and group agents*. Oxford: Oxford University Press.

Veldman, J., & Willmott, H. (2017). Social ontology and the modern corporation. *Cambridge Journal of Economics, 41*(5), 1489–1504. doi:10.1093/cje/bex043

Witt, C. (2011). *The metaphysics of gender*. Oxford: Oxford University Press.

Witt, C. (2023). *Social goodness: The ontology of social norms*: Oxford University Press.

2 Totalities and their components

Underpinning social positioning theory is the assessment that there is a level of commonality to the constitution of all phenomena.[1] This commonality is that both social and non-social phenomena are everywhere constituted through processes that (re)produce and/or transform totalities. These processes are ones whereby sets of pre-existing elements or items come to be relationally organised.[2] Lawson refers to these relationally organised elements as components. Totalities, then, are systems of components. In short, "the forming of totalities by way of various existing items becoming organised in a manner as to form their components is not peculiar to the social realm, [. . .] it is a feature of seemingly all domains of reality"[3] (Lawson, 2022, p. 3).

The pre-existing elements that become organised—giving rise to the components of totalities—are often also themselves totalities. The picture, therefore, is one in which "reality everywhere, from quantum fields to the social domain, consists of emergent totalities formed as organisations of pre-existing elements, with such emergent totalities themselves in turn becoming very often organised as components of higher level totalities" (Lawson, 2016c, p. 447). So, phenomena are commonly constituted through the organisation of other previously constituted totalities in other domains of reality. Indeed, social totalities are often constituted through the organisation of non-social totalities. Therefore, this conception is thoroughly naturalistic.[4]

The aim in this chapter is to consider the nature of totalities and their components in general terms. Key, here, is recognising the importance of organisation.[5] I begin, therefore, by illustrating the role that organisation plays in the constitution of all totalities. Once the role of organisation is recognised, two central features of all totalities so constituted become clear, which I consider in turn. The first is that both totalities and their components are irreducible to the elements out of which they are constituted. The second is that totalities operate through the workings of their components.[6] Finally, I provide a clarification as to Lawson's use of the term emergence, which has at times been misinterpreted as an explanatory feature of his framework.

DOI: 10.4324/9781003110873-2

Organisation

To understand the role of organisation in the constitution of totalities, it is helpful to consider the constitution of a familiar totality, say—as Lawson typically does—the construction of a building that could be used as a house. Here, the pre-existing elements might include "bricks, mortar, wood, panes of glass, cement" with "a context, a plot of land" (Lawson, 2013a, p. 64). Constitution then occurs through a process of construction in which these pre-existing elements are organised in relation to one another, which results in the formation of components of the emerging totality. For example, a pre-existing element such as a pane of glass might be relationally organised by being placed within a frame within a hole in a wall giving rise to a component such as a window.

At "any stage in the process of construction, an observer will find not only the part of the building constructed so far [. . .] but also the relational organisation of the latter" where "this organisation will be essential to the house's construction and properties" (Lawson, 2013a, p. 64). And when the construction of the building is completed, so is the relational organisation of the pre-existing elements through which they are formed into components, "the two—the totality and the organisational structure—emerge simultaneously" (Lawson, 2013a, p. 64). So, organisation is central to such a constitutive process. Indeed, imagine that the building is dismantled and the pre-existing elements are arranged in some random fashion. It is very unlikely that the randomly arranged materials would constitute a house. So, the organisation makes a difference.

In other words, the building is not a building until all of the elements are organised in a particular way. The building would not be a building were the elements used to be arranged randomly. Indeed, it is only when their organisation takes a specific form that the building possesses the causal properties of a house, such as being able to provide shelter. The totality— the building—and the particular organisation of a set of elements come into being simultaneously. The building would not be constituted were it not for its organisational structure and, therefore, the organisation itself makes a difference. In short, the "organising structure, a feature that is external and additional to the items laid out in a row, matters. It makes a difference to any resulting construction and its properties, determining that and how the items incorporated make a contribution" (Lawson, 2022, p. 3). Lawson's assessment is that organisation plays an equivalent role in the constitution of all totalities, from "quantum fields to the social domain".

Irreducibility

Totalities so constituted, as well as their components, are ontologically and causally irreducible to the pre-existing elements out of which they are constituted.[7] By ontologically irreducible, I mean that the nature of a particular component is not reducible to the nature of the element out of which it is formed and consequently the nature of the totality is not reducible to the natures of the collection of pre-existing elements out of which its components are formed. By causally irreducible, I mean that the capacities of the components and the totality to make a difference are not reducible to those of the pre-existing elements. Both forms of irreducibility are explained by the additional constitutive role, and ensuing causal impact, of organisation.

Continuing with the example of the construction of a building that might be used as a house, let us first consider ontological and causal irreducibility at the level of a component. Take, for example, a window. As explained earlier, in this example, the component—window—is formed when a pre-existing element—a pane of glass—is organised in a particular set of relations such as being placed within a frame within a hole within the wall of a building. In this case, the component window is made up of the pane of glass and the particular form of relational organisation to which it is subjected. The component is both the pre-existing element and the organisation. So, the component is ontologically irreducible to the pre-existing element because the nature of the component—constituted of the pre-existing element and the organisation—is distinct from the nature of the pre-existing element separate from those relations. The window is not the same thing as the pane of glass.

The component, then, is causally irreducible to the pre-existing element because the way in which such a window makes a difference is different from the way in which a pane of glass makes a difference. This window, for example, lets light into a building without also letting in wind and rain. A pane of glass lying on the ground may well have the capacity to let light through it, but it does not stop wind or rain unless it is placed in relation to other materials. So, the causal capacities of the window are not the same as the causal capacities of the pane of glass, precisely because the component also includes the organisation, which makes a difference. In short, "the components of any totality [. . .] have relational features that are not possessed by the items or phenomena used in producing them" (Lawson, 2022, p. 3). Therefore, components so formed are both ontologically and causally irreducible.

It then follows that totalities are also both ontologically and causally irreducible to the pre-existing elements, considered apart from being organised. The totality, the building, is made up of components. Indeed, it is nothing more than its components, given that the components include both the pre-existing elements and the organisation. The totality—the building—therefore, is ontologically irreducible because it is not the same thing as the disorganised building materials. As underlined earlier, the same building materials used to constitute the house laid out randomly or in a row do not constitute a building. Without the formation of components occurring through a process of relational organisation, there is no building. So, the nature of the building is not the same, is not reducible, to the disorganised building materials out of which it is constituted. It is then clearly also the case that the way in which the building makes a difference is not the same as the way in which the disorganised building materials make a difference. A building can, for example, provide shelter. A set of building materials arranged randomly is very unlikely to provide shelter in the same way. Indeed, for Lawson (2013a, p. 64), as it is "unlikely the outcome would have the causal powers of a house", the organisation makes a difference and so "on this criterion of causality, i.e., of possessing the power or ability to make a difference, the relational organisation is causal".[8]

Irreducibility, both ontological and causal, then, is a central feature of all totalities and their components so constituted.[9] This irreducibility is explained "simply because organisation always makes a difference and must be recognised as an essential feature of the totality" (Lawson, 2022, p. 3). Indeed, organisation is both an essential feature of the totality and of a totality's components, and both, therefore, are ontologically and causally irreducible.[10]

Ways of working

Totalities work or operate through the operation or working of their components. Totalities do not work separately from their components nor do they act upon them.[11] Indeed, as identified earlier, a totality is not separate from its components, "for the former is composed out of the latter" (Lawson, 2013a, p. 80). Here, once again, organisation is key. For once it is recognised that the components of totalities are made up of both the pre-existing elements and their organisation then one can see clearly that a totality is nothing but its components. Therefore, totalities can only operate through the workings of their components.[12]

Take, again, the building that could be used as a house. One way in which the totality—the building—could work could be to provide shelter. The question, then, is how does the building provide shelter? It does so, as already alluded to earlier, precisely because the pre-existing elements, the bricks, mortar, panes of glass etc. are organised in a particular way. Through this organisation these elements give rise to components. The building, the totality, then provides shelter through its components—the windows, the doors, the roof, etc.—working. There is no sense in which the building provides shelter in a manner that is separate from its windows and roof nor does the building somehow act upon the windows and roof to provide shelter.[13]

Alternatively, Lawson (2022, p. 3) explains that a "football team wins through its players scoring more goals than they concede; a rock band produces its music through its members performing". Or, for Lawson (2014, p. 6), "an army attacks through the actions of its soldiers (or guided weapons); a school educates through the interactions of its members" and even "[a]n individual picks up a pen through the various interactions of the brain, nervous system, muscles, etc.". That is not, however, to say that the elements out of which the components are formed have no bearing at all on the working of the totality. Indeed, as Lawson explains:

> [T]he capacities of components, though not reducible to, do include, those of the elements out of which they are formed. So, the properties of the elements organised can bear on the workings of the totality; but they do so, and can only do so, through the workings of the components formed out of them, the basic elements bear on how the components can perform.
>
> (Lawson, 2022, p. 4)

Take again the example of a window as a component of a building used as a house that has as its way of working providing shelter. Although it is clear that it is through the component window and its relationship to all of the other components of the totality that shelter can be provided, the capacities of the pane of glass—say transparency and being solid—contribute to this way of working insofar as they contribute to the capacities of the component window to let in light without also letting in wind and rain. So, as the capacities of the components include the capacities of the elements that come to be organised, these elements can and do contribute to the workings of totalities but only insofar as their capacities contribute to those of components. Totalities, in all cases, operate through the workings of their components.

The above covers the principles that apply generally to all totalities and their components. However, I consider it to be important to make a brief point of clarification before concluding this chapter. For a concept, which I have not mentioned earlier, is often mischaracterised as being central to Lawson's understanding of the general features of the constitution of totalities. That concept is emergence.[14]

Emergence

Unfortunately, on the constitution and nature of totalities, Lawson has often been misunderstood. The key mistake has been to suppose that, for Lawson, the concept most central is that of emergence.[15] It is therefore helpful to briefly clarify how the term emergence is employed by Lawson.

For Lawson, the term *emergence* is interpreted as little more than a placeholder.[16] It refers just to the appearance of novelty; its use marks the spot where something new arises out of what already existed. Therefore, "[e]mergence [. . .] is not an explanatory term, but rather one that marks the spots where (diachronic) explanatory work remains to be undertaken" (Lawson, 2012, p. 348). Indeed, Lawson considers that the term emergence is regularly made to do far more than it is able to, obscuring the further explanatory work that remains to be done.[17]

To be clear then, Lawson uses the term *emerge* as a synonym to *arise* or *come into being*. It is deployed to indicate that a process is occurring through which novelty appears. When Lawson refers to a totality as an emergent totality, it is the same as saying a novel totality. Lawson has used the terms emerge and emergent because his arguments have often been developed in debates regarding emergence.[18] In these debates, the central issue for Lawson has usually been whether emergent phenomena are reducible in some way. As shown earlier, where the emergent phenomenon is a totality formed by organising pre-existing elements, Lawson rejects common notions of causal and ontological reductionism.

So, Lawson is focused on how totalities and, in particular, social totalities, are constituted. He is not developing a theory of emergence as a causal factor. Rather, as I have made clear earlier, the key to understanding this constitutive process, Lawson argues, is organisation. Organisation, not emergence, is the central category in Lawson's account.

Concluding remarks

Phenomena are everywhere constituted where pre-existing elements, which are often themselves totalities, become relationally organised to form components of other totalities. As such, the conception of social ontology defended in Cambridge attributes a level of commonality to the constitution of social and non-social phenomena. In all cases, organisation and the totality come into being simultaneously.

Totalities and their components cannot be reduced, either causally or ontologically, to the elements that are to be organised to form components, if considered apart from being organised. For the organising structure makes an ontological and causal contribution. Moreover, totalities are consequently nothing more than their components and as such operate through the workings of their components and so cannot simultaneous act back either on these components or on the elements out of which they are organisationally constituted.

Central to this assessment is the recognition that organisation applies at all levels of reality. Indeed, all totalities come into being through organisation and this must be recognised if we are to understand how they are constituted. So, all questions relating to the constitution of totalities essentially reduce to questions of how these phenomena are, and have come to be, organised:

> [W]hether social or not [. . .], the various sorts of elements that come to form components of novel totalities have somehow to bind together. In the non-social world this binding may happen by way of processes of chemical bonding, electrical attraction, collision etc. In the social

case constitutive social relations are always involved, where these emerge through individual processes of social positioning.

(Lawson, 2019, p. 12)

My focus, then, is specifically on how social totalities are and have come to be organised—on these processes of social positioning. But which totalities are social? I turn now to answering this question with a view to clearly demarcating which totalities' constitution social positioning theory aims to explain.

Notes

1 I follow Lawson in employing the term phenomenon as a generic ontological category, using it, in particular, when referring to all phenomena or when distinguishing, as I do in later chapters, between social and non-social phenomena.

2 Lawson (2012, p. 357) takes care to note that this is always an ongoing process, as "[i]f emergent organisation is seemingly characteristic of all reality, and if features of reality are continually being reorganised (as well as de- or disorganised), it appears that everything is effectively in process".

3 Lawson previously expressed this idea by explaining:

> A *totality* is a system of organised, usually more basic and pre-existing, elements that reveals a coherence or integrity at the system level. Totalities emerge through the *relational organisation* (perhaps with some modification) of these pre-existing elements, the latter thereby being harnessed and organised as *components* [. . .].
>
> (Lawson, 2014, p. 3)

4 I acknowledge that the term naturalism has a variety of meanings. I follow Lawson in using the term ontological naturalism to refer to:

> [T]he widely accepted doctrine that everything can be explained in terms of natural causes. This is a non-dualist orientation that entails that even features such as life, choice and intentionality are integrated with the (rest of the) natural world and not composed of some separate (non-naturalistic) stuff.
>
> (Lawson, 2012, p. 346)

Lawson's explicit emphasis on ontological naturalism in his more recent contributions seems to have come about, at least in part, as a consequence of his intellectual engagement with Searle. A major concern for Searle relates to establishing how:

> The higher level phenomena of mind and society are dependent on lower level phenomena of physics and biology: Biology depends on physics. Neurobiology is a branch of biology. Consciousness and intentionality are caused by and realized in neurobiology. Collective intentionality is a type of intentionality, and society is created by collective intentionality.
>
> (Searle, 2010, p. 25)

Lawson has acknowledged that in his early work he had perhaps not been explicit enough in grounding the ontological conception he was developing as naturalistic:

> If [. . .] I have given insufficient explicit attention to ontological naturalism in previous contributions, the latter, as I say, is nevertheless a thesis

I broadly accept. My previous neglect of a naturalistic assessment of my position is, thus, to repeat, something I seek explicitly to rectify here.
(Lawson, 2012, p. 348)

In establishing the naturalistic credentials of his project, Lawson also seems to provide a fuller account than that which Searle offers by explaining that there are common features to the constitution of all phenomena.

5 I acknowledge that the term organisation is used in a variety of ways within many literatures, including a whole field of organisational studies. For a comparison of Lawson's use of the term with other similar uses, see Pratten (2019). Moreover, Lawson discusses a possible ambiguity in the use of the term organisation:

I should perhaps quickly note here that the term organisation has two inflections. In processes of emergence the lower-level elements become organised as components of the emergent entity or whole, and so we can refer to the organisation of the components. But the category organisation is also regularly employed to refer to the totality including the lower-level elements that have become (re)organised. Hopefully it will be clear from context which meaning is intended here. When the term refers to the emergent entity or totality, i.e. when organisation is a whole or a system, then it includes not just the lower-level elements that (perhaps with or through modification) have become components, along with their context, but also an organising structure comprising emergent relations between components (as well, of course, others that bind these components to features in their environment).
(Lawson, 2012, p. 352)

Lawson explains that this ambiguity in the use of the term has, in the context of discussions of the nature of the firm, generated significant problems:

In fact the reference to the firm as an organisation itself encourages problems, just because the term "organisation", when so used, denotes, for the contributions in questions, *both* the totality itself as well as its relational (organising) structure. As we have seen, the two, the totality and its organising structure, emerge simultaneously but are not identical. In social theory more widely the use of the term "organisation" in this dual manner leads often to the two features (the totality and its relational structure) being conflated, usually with one or the other feature consequently being neglected.
(Lawson, 2014, p. 6)

Here, I do not use the term organisation to refer to the totality. I use the term organisation to refer to the relational organising structure of a totality.

6 This assessment is in opposition to the idea that totalities might act down upon their constitutive parts, which is generally referred to as downward causation. There are a number of different conceptions of downward causation. For useful overviews of the literature and debates related to downward causation, see Elder-Vass (2010, 2012b); Hodgson (2002, 2007, 2011); Hulswit (2005) and Kim (1992, 1999, 2000). Lawson (2013a, p. 79) has specifically contested a conception that "understands 'downward causation [. . .] [as] the concept that a system as a whole has a causal influence on its constitutive parts' [. . .], that 'higher level entities causally affect their lower-level constituents'", a definition he takes from Hulswit (2005, p. 261). But, in fact, Lawson (2013a, p. 63) "doubt[s] whether the conception of downward causation as formulated has any relevance whatsoever". Moreover, Pratten (2013, p. 265) notes that "Lawson's own preference is to avoid the current common confusions

in the literature by dropping altogether reference to downward causation". I, therefore, have chosen to avoid employing the terminology of downward causation in the body of this chapter.

7 This assessment is in opposition to arguments in favour of causal reduction. There are two distinct theses regarding causal reduction that Lawson has considered. The first, which Lawson characterises as simplistic, argues in effect that the causal powers of an emergent totality are reducible to the causal powers of the items to be organised as components, considered apart from being so organised. This conception ignores the causal role of a totality's organising structure. When a totality is constituted through the relational organisation of pre-existing elements resulting in the formation of components, the causal influence of the organisation is something that is additional to the pre-existing elements. It is not the case that the pre-existing elements are simply aggregated such that the causal powers of the totality are merely an addition of those elements. Rather, the causal properties of the totality are the product of the elements organised and the organisational structure. Therefore, this simplistic version of causal reduction does not hold.

The second formulation is associated with Searle, who argues:

Causal Reduction [. . .] is a relation between any two types of things that can have causal powers, where the existence and a fortiori the causal powers of the reduced entity are shown to be entirely explainable in terms of the causal powers of the reducing phenomena. Thus, for example, some objects are solid and this has causal consequences: solid objects are impenetrable by other objects, they are resistant to pressure, etc. But these causal powers can be causally explained by the causal powers of vibratory movements of molecules in lattice structures.

(Searle, 1992, p. 114)

For Lawson:

Searle is in fact advancing an epistemological notion of causal reduction; the latter is couched in explanatory terms. In consequence, it may be suggested that Searle is merely observing (correctly) that a diachronic explanatory account of all higher level entities can be provided. But in his suggesting that the existence and causal powers of the emergent entity are "entirely explainable" in terms of the causal powers of the "reducing" phenomena, Searle is advancing a more strongly reductionist position than this. If it is generally the case that [. . .] the organising structure of components makes a causal contribution to the powers of the whole (and I shall suggest that this is so), then Searle's notion of causal reduction seems to require that the organisational structure is also explained (produced) solely by the causal interactions of the lower level components. Only where this is so can it be held that Searle's notion of causal reduction is at least feasible.

(Lawson, 2013a, p. 65)

In fact, Lawson (2014, p. 3) does identify at least one instance in which he thinks this occurs, but he stresses that "even this version of the thesis [of causal reduction] does not hold in most cases and seems never to with respect to social causation". The sort of mechanism that Lawson has in mind here is one wherein a totality is formed out of pre-existing items via "processes of mutual cancelling" between these elements that occasionally results in an organised entity as residue. In such cases, it can be argued that any "organising structure of interacting elements that remains was brought about by the interaction of those elements alone as part of a constructive process of order creation" (Lawson, 2013a,

p. 68). Specifically, Lawson (2013a, p. 69) argues that this is the case with surface tension—"a property of the surface of a liquid matter whereby the latter gives resistance to an external object"—as:

> [T]here is reason to suggest that both the emergent property of surface tension, along with the emergent structure of the drop of liquid upon which the former depends, result from the interaction of the component molecules alone. Here Searle's notion of causal reduction seems relevant. Notice that the internal organising structure of the molecules emerges at the same time as do liquid properties like surface tension.
>
> (Lawson, 2013a, p. 69)

Lawson, however, argues that when the constitution of non-social phenomena involves even a slightly more complex organisational process than cancelling, causal reduction no longer occurs. For more, see (Lawson, 2013a).

8 Lawson has, at times, drawn on Aristotle's four causes to distinguish the type of causation he associates with organisation from that which he associates with the totality. Lawson has termed the way in which the totality and the organising structure are causal "efficient" and "formal", respectively. With regard to the house example, Lawson (2013a, p. 64) has argued that totalities have powers of efficient causation in the sense that a house can "provide safety and shelter, [. . .] facilitate family or other indoor activities, [. . .] be bought and sold, and so on". In referring to the causal powers of the totality's organising structure as an example of formal causation, Lawson (2013a, p. 64) means how the organisation of the components "makes the house feasible". While Lawson does not include material and final cause in this example, he has discussed them elsewhere. For a discussion of final causation, see Lawson (2013a, p. 77). For his use of material cause, see Lawson (1997, p. 31; 2003, p. 149). Other members of the Cambridge Social Ontology Group have analysed different ways in which the four causes can be used to understand social phenomena. For more, see Lewis (2000); Martins (2011) and Pratten (2009).

9 Lawson draws upon this irreducibility to ground the objects of study of the different sciences. Indeed, Lawson's view is that a class of phenomena deserves to be an object of study if it can be shown to be irreducible. And Lawson (2012, p. 359) argues that "all forms of established science have objects of study that are synchronically irreducible". The reasoning is that if a phenomenon is irreducible it would need to be explained in its own right and not in terms of the pre-existing elements that come to be organised to form its components. Irreducible phenomena can only be understood by studying those phenomena. They cannot be reduced, or explained, in terms of others. Lawson draws on this argument, in particular, to justify that an autonomous social science is possible and warranted:

> What would it take to demonstrate [. . .] that a meaningful social science is [. . .] entirely feasible? A sufficient response, I take it, would be to identify causal factors, properties or/and entities that can reasonably be categorised as *social*, which possess their own distinct mode of being, yet are as real or objective as the objects studied within the traditional "natural" sciences, and in a relevant sense irreducible to the latter. [. . .] I contend that, whatever the achievements of "social science" to date, the material conditions for a social science that is scientific in the sense of existing natural science are entirely present.
>
> (Lawson, 2012, p. 346)

I consider the meaning of the term social and the phenomena consequently demarcated in detail in the following chapter.

10 This is a very different treatment of organisation than say Searle. Searle (2016, p. 406), for example, treats organisation as always being bound up with the elements that get organised, noting that "[w]hen the physicist says the table can be reduced to the molecules, he means to include the organization of the molecules". Whether or not physicists consider things this way, Lawson responds by explaining:

> Why do I not consign the organisation of the elements along with the latter to the "base"? My answer is simply because the organising structure is, and is always, itself an emergent. Whether the focus is on the formation of physical liquids or solids, or social artefacts [. . .], the totality emerges along with, and through the emergence of, its organising structure.
>
> (Lawson, 2016d, p. 431)

11 As noted in a previous footnote, the idea that the totality acts down upon its components is generally referred to as downward causation. Interestingly, Pratten (2013, p. 265) has argued that Lawson "at times [. . .] defend[s] an account of downward causation that respects the distinction drawn between emergent totality and organising structure". For there is a causal interaction between the elements that become organised and so form components and the organisational relational structure. Thus, when human individuals become organised say as components of a crowd, then, according to Lawson:

> The individuals in their interactions draw not on the crowd behaviour as a totality, but on the relational structures that organises individuals as components of the crowd. And it is through these same interactions of relationally organised individuals that the relational structures are in turn reproduced and/or transformed. In short, causal interaction is between individuals and organising structure.
>
> (Lawson, 2013a, p. 81)

Lawson is careful not to imply that such an interaction is deterministic:

> Any causal bearing that even the organisational structure has on human practices is causation in the sense not of "bringing about" individual practices such as, say, speech acts, but of shaping them through serving as conditions of their possibility. For, of course, organisational structures are not somehow able to bear down on the individual in some external unmediated fashion. It is human beings that do things, so that everything that happens in the social world does so through human activity.
>
> (Lawson, 2013a, p. 82)

Pratten (2013, p. 265) has also argued that interactivist conceptions of downward causation are perhaps compatible with Lawson's views.

Lawson (2013a, p. 82) agrees that interaction of the sort described earlier could perhaps be referred to as a type of downward causation, if the organising structure, being emergent is considered thereby to be "higher level'. For debates relating to downward causation are generally framed in terms of a "higher level" acting down upon a "lower level". But levels, after all, are a metaphor. So, if one were to consider the upper level to be the organisation and the lower level to be the items organised to form components, a form of downward causation would hold. On the criterion of novelty, however, the higher level would include the totality, the organisation and the components. In that case, as a totality acts through its components acting, all of this would occur at the higher level, meaning that downward causation would not hold.

12 Lawson has at times illustrated this argument using the terminology of parts and wholes:

> [W]holes act through their parts acting and their parts are coordinated in their actions through the emergent irreducible relational structures that organise the lower level elements as (perhaps through modification) components of emergent wholes.[. . .] Parts of a whole though interact with, and relate directly to, not a whole but each other and the organising structure.
>
> (Lawson, 2014, p. 6)

In Lawson's use of the term "part", it is not always clear if he is referring to the component or the pre-existing elements. Therefore, I have chosen to avoid this terminology in the body of this chapter.

13 Were I to employ the terminology of higher-level and lower-level phenomena for this example, the lower level would include all of the materials such as "bricks, mortar, wood, panes of glass, cement, etc." as well as the "context, a plot of land", before they get organised. The higher level would then include those novel features that come into being once those elements are organised and formed into components. The higher level, therefore, includes the totality—the building—its organisational structure and the components. So, while the pre-existing elements can be considered lower-level phenomena, once they are organised to give rise to components, then these components are themselves part of the higher level. Therefore, there is no sense in which the higher level can act down on the lower level.

14 For an overview and history of the notion of emergence, see, for example, Cahoone (2013) and Gibb, Hendry, and Lancaster (2019).

15 Perhaps surprisingly, given his sustained engagement with Lawson's contributions, this claim has been made most notably by John Searle. Indeed, Searle thinks that Lawson interprets emergence as an explanatory concept. Searle argues that while "[t]he concept and the application of the concept of emergence is the centerpiece of Lawson's account", in fact "the notion of emergence plays no explanatory role" in Lawson's actual analysis (Searle, 2016, pp. 404–405). If Searle is right in identifying that emergence, for Lawson, is not explanatory, he is wrong to think that this is a critique of Lawson's position. Emergence, as explained earlier, is not the centrepiece of Lawson's account, and Lawson indeed acknowledges that the term is not explanatory.

That said, Searle has written extensively on emergence and seems to have a rather different understanding of the term to Lawson. Searle argues that emergence necessarily leads to both ontological and causal reductions, except in the case of consciousness where he argues:

> [T]he traditional account of consciousness as emergent, in the sense explained, cannot be made philosophically rigorous and coherent. But the picture is clear enough. Here is the brain with all its brainy features and here is consciousness with all of its amazing features. Consciousness is dependent on the brain and emerges from brain activities, but it cannot be reduced to the brain or brain processes. In this sense consciousness is emergent.
>
> (Searle, 2016, p. 405)

Consciousness, he argues, is, therefore, distinct and unable to be *reduced* to the brain and those organised processes and therefore is ontologically irreducible. For more on Searle's conception of emergence and its relationship to questions of reducibility, see Lawson (2016d) and Searle (1992, 1995, 2016). Another example of attributing undue importance to Lawson's understanding of emergence is provided by Wight, who argues:

The manner in which Lawson treats emergence means that almost anything that comes into being through the interaction of one or more things
can be said to be emergent. Thus, if I meet a friend in the street, the conversation we have emerges out of the chance meeting. The conversation
was previously absent, it came out of, although it is still dependent upon,
matters (myself and my friend) already in existence. This is a very loose
and certainly not philosophically interesting use of emergence.

(Wight, 2016, p. 417)

16 I acknowledge that in earlier work, Lawson presents the theme of emergence
somewhat differently from the way he sets it out more recently. Indeed, in earlier contributions, he seems to use the term emergence in a manner very much
in line with its deployment in the broad literature on critical realism without too
much elaboration. For example, Lawson (1997, p. 63) writes that "[e]mergence
may be defined as a relationship between two features or aspects such that one
arises out of the other and yet, while perhaps being capable of reacting back on
it, remains causally and taxonomically irreducible to it". Or, in more detail:

A stratum of reality can be said to be emergent, or as possessing emergent powers, if there is a sense in which it (i) has arisen out of a lower
stratum, being formed by principles operative at the lower level; (ii) remains dependent on the lower stratum for its existence; but (iii) contains
causal powers of its own which are irreducible to those operating at the
lower level and (perhaps) capable of acting back on the lower level. Thus
organic material emerged from inorganic material. And, according to the
conception I am defending, the social realm is emergent from human (in-
ter)action, though with properties irreducible to, yet capable of causally
affecting, the latter.

(Lawson, 2003, pp. 43–44)

These definitions are characterised not only by the idea of novelty but also
by the importance placed on the relationships that exist between emergent
phenomena and their constitutive components, namely causal irreducibility.
For more on the critical realist conception of emergence, see Bhaskar (2008
[1975], 2009 [1986], 2015 [1979]) and Collier (1994). Moreover, when it comes to
emergence Bhaskar and critical realist contributors more generally have been
influenced by the work of von Bertalanffy (1950, 2015) and Polanyi (2009). For
more on the relationship between critical realism and Systems Theory, see,
for example, Carchedi (1983); Hofkirchner (2019) and Mingers (2011). There
has also been a substantial amount of research on emergence conducted from
other perspectives that are related to both critical realism and Cambridge
social ontology. See, for example, Archer (2013, 2014, 2015, 2016, 2017) and
Elder-Vass (2010, 2012a, 2012b, 2014).

17 This is a view that is seemingly shared, for example, by Piaget (1970) and Bechtel and Richardson (2010). For example, Piaget writes:

The whole which this sort of critic of atomism posits at the outset is
viewed as the outcome of some sort of emergence, vaguely conceived as
a law of nature and not further analysed. Thus, when Comte proposed to
explain men in terms of humanity, not humanity in terms of men, or when
Durkheim thought of the social whole as emerging from the union of individuals in much the same way as molecules are formed by the union
of atoms, or when the Gestalt psychologists believed they could discern
immediate wholes in primary perception comparable to the field effects
that figure in electromagnetism, they did indeed remind us that a whole
is not the same as a simple juxtaposition of previously available elements,

and for this they deserve our gratitude; but by viewing the whole as prior to its elements or contemporaneous with their "contact", they simplified the problem to such an extent as to risk bypassing the central questions— questions about the nature of a whole's laws of composition.

(Piaget, 1970, p. 8)

Piaget also argues that:

The same holds for the theory of emergence defended by Lloyd Morgan and others; to note the existence of wholes at different levels and to re- mark that at a given moment the higher "emerges" from the lower is to locate a problem, not to solve it.

(Piaget, 1970, p. 46)

For more, see Santos (2015).

18 Perhaps confusion has arisen because of such a context and the fact that Law- son regularly wrote of how all phenomena emerge through the organisation of some set of pre-existing elements. For example, Lawson writes:

I use the term emergence primarily to capture any processes whereby some pre-existing elements become organised into a totality or system, a system that is novel or unprecedented in relation to those elements and their context. In addition, I use the term emergent in reference to the total- ity itself, its causal properties, and the organisation of the elements.

(Lawson, 2016d, pp. 429–430)

A further example is where Lawson (2013a, p. 62) writes "[e]mergence then, as widely interpreted, is ultimately a compositional term, and one that involves components being organised rather than aggregated". More recently, he notes:

Reality everywhere (for the social and the non-social alike) is marked by specific processes of emergence. These are processes whereby various elements in existence at any given point in time become relationally or- ganised to form components of some novel or 'emergent' totality, with the latter in turn perhaps becoming in due course itself organised as a component of a yet higher-level totality and so on.

(Lawson, 2019, p. 12)

It is also the case that in almost every instance in which Lawson has discussed organisation it has come under the heading of emergence. See, for example Lawson (2012, 2013a, 2013b, 2016a, 2016b, 2016c); Lewis (2015); Martins (2011); Porpora (2017); Pratten (2013); Searle (2016) and Wight (2016).

References

Archer, M. S. (Ed.) (2013). *Social morphogenesis*. Dordrecht: Springer.

Archer, M. S. (Ed.) (2014). *Late modernity: Trajectories towards morphogenic society.* Dordrecht: Springer.

Archer, M. S. (Ed.) (2015). *Generative mechanisms transforming the social order.* Dordrecht: Springer.

Archer, M. S. (Ed.) (2016). *Morphogenesis and the crisis of normativity.* Dordrecht: Springer.

Archer, M. S. (Ed.) (2017). *Morphogenesis and human flourishing.* Dordrecht: Springer.

Bechtel, W., & Richardson, R. C. (2010). *Discovering complexity: Decomposition and localization as strategies in scientific research.* Cambridge: MIT Press.

Bhaskar, R. (2008 [1975]). *A realist theory of science.* London and New York: Routledge.

Bhaskar, R. (2009 [1986]). *Scientific realism and human emancipation*. London and New York: Routledge.

Bhaskar, R. (2015 [1979]). *The possibility of naturalism: A philosophical critique of the contemporary human sciences*. London and New York: Routledge.

Cahoone, L. E. (2013). *The orders of nature*. Albany: State University of New York Press.

Carchedi, G. (1983). A critical note on Bhaskar and systems theory. *Radical Philosophy* (33), 27–30.

Collier, A. (1994). *Critical realism: An introduction to Roy Bhaskar's philosophy*. London and New York: Verso.

Elder-Vass, D. (2010). *The causal power of social structures: Emergence, structure and agency*. Cambridge: Cambridge University Press.

Elder-Vass, D. (2012a). *The reality of social construction*. Cambridge: Cambridge University Press.

Elder-Vass, D. (2012b). Top-down causation and social structures. *Interface Focus*, 2(1), 82–90. doi:10.1098/rsfs.2011.0055

Elder-Vass, D. (2014). Social emergence: Functional or relational. *Balkan Journal of Philosophy*, 6(1), 5–16.

Gibb, S., Hendry, R. F., & Lancaster, T. (Eds.). (2019). *The Routledge handbook of emergence*. London and New York: Routledge.

Hodgson, G. M. (2002). Reconstitutive downward causation: Social structure and the development of individual agency. In E. Fullbrook (Ed.), *Intersubjectivity in economics: Agents and structures* (pp. 159–181). London and New York: Routledge.

Hodgson, G. M. (2007). Institutions and individuals: Interaction and evolution. *Organization Studies*, 28(1), 95–116. doi:10.1177/0170840607067832

Hodgson, G. M. (2011). *Downward causation—some second thoughts*. Retrieved from www.geoffreymhodgson.uk/downward-causation

Hofkirchner, W. (2019). Social relations: Building on Ludwig von Bertalanffy. *Systems Research and Behavioral Science*, 1–11. doi:10.1002/sres.2594

Hulswit, M. (2005). How causal is downward causation? *Journal for General Philosophy of Science*, 36(2), 261–287. doi:10.1007/s10838-006-7153-3

Kim, J. (1992). "Downward causation" in emergentism and nonreductive physicalism. In A. Beckermann, H. Flohr, & J. Kim (Eds.), *Emergence or reduction?: Essays on the prospects of nonreductive physicalism* (pp. 119–138). Berlin and New York: Walter De Gruyter.

Kim, J. (1999). Making sense of emergence. *Philosophical Studies*, 95(1), 3–36. doi:10.1023/a:1004563122154

Kim, J. (2000). Making sense of downward causation. In P. B. Andersen, C. Emmeche, N. O. Finnemann, & P. V. Christiansen (Eds.), *Downward causation* (pp. 305–321). Aarhus: University of Aarhus Press.

Lawson, T. (1997). *Economics and reality*. London and New York: Routledge.

Lawson, T. (2003). *Reorienting economics*. London and New York: Routledge.

Lawson, T. (2012). Ontology and the study of social reality: Emergence, organisation, community, power, social relations, corporations, artefacts and money. *Cambridge Journal of Economics*, 36(2), 345–385. doi:10.1093/cje/ber050

Lawson, T. (2013a). Emergence and morphogenesis: Causal reduction and downward causation? In M. S. Archer (Ed.), *Social morphogenesis* (pp. 61–85). Dordrecht: Springer.

Lawson, T. (2013b). Emergence and social causation. In R. Groff & J. Greco (Eds.), *Powers and capacities in philosophy: The new Aristotelianism* (pp. 285–308). London and New York: Routledge.

Lawson, T. (2014). The nature of the firm and peculiarities of the corporation. *Cambridge Journal of Economics*, 39(1), 1–32. doi:10.1093/cje/beu046

Lawson, T. (2016a). Collective practices and norms. In M. S. Archer (Ed.), *Morphogenesis and the crisis of normativity* (pp. 249–279). Dordrecht: Springer.

Lawson, T. (2016b). Comparing conceptions of social ontology: Emergent social entities and/or institutional facts? *Journal for the Theory of Social Behaviour, 46*(4), 359–399. doi:10.1111/jtsb.12126

Lawson, T. (2016c). Ontology and social relations: Reply to Doug Porpora and to Colin Wight. *Journal for the Theory of Social Behaviour, 46*(4), 438–449. doi:10.1111/jtsb.12128

Lawson, T. (2016d). Some critical issues in social ontology: Reply to John Searle. *Journal for the Theory of Social Behaviour, 46*(4), 426–437.

Lawson, T. (2019). *The nature of social reality: Issues in social ontology*. London and New York: Routledge.

Lawson, T. (2022). Social positioning theory. *Cambridge Journal of Economics, 46*(1), 1–39. doi:10.1093/cje/beab040

Lewis, P. (2000). Realism, causality and the problem of social structure. *Journal for the Theory of Social Behaviour, 30*(3), 249–268. doi:10.1111/1468–5914.00129

Lewis, P. (2015). Notions of order and process in Hayek: The significance of emergence. *Cambridge Journal of Economics, 39*(4), 1167–1190. doi:10.1093/cje/beu043

Martins, N. O. (2011). An evolutionary approach to emergence and social causation. *Journal of Critical Realism, 10*(2), 192–218. doi:10.1558/jcr.v10i2.192

Mingers, J. (2011). The contribution of systemic thought to critical realism. *Journal of Critical Realism, 10*(3), 303–330. doi:10.1558/jcr.v10i3.303

Piaget, J. (1970). *Structuralism*. New York: Basic Books.

Polanyi, M. (2009). *The tacit dimension*. Chicago; London: University of Chicago Press.

Porpora, D. (2017). Tony Lawson from a sociological point of view. *Cambridge Journal of Economics, 41*(5), 1525–1537. doi:10.1093/cje/bex032

Pratten, S. (2009). Critical realism and causality: Tracing the Aristotelian legacy. *Journal for the Theory of Social Behaviour, 39*(2), 189–218. doi:10.1111/j.1468–5914.2009.00400.x

Pratten, S. (2013). Critical realism and the process account of emergence. *Journal for the Theory of Social Behaviour, 43*(3), 251–279. doi:doi:10.1111/jtsb.12017

Pratten, S. (2019). Dewey on organisation. *European Journal of Pragmatism and American Philosophy, XI*(2). doi:10.4000/ejpap.1671

Santos, G. C. (2015). Ontological emergence: How is that possible? Towards a new relational ontology. *Foundations of Science, 20*(4), 429–446. doi:10.1007/s10699–015–9419-x

Searle, J. R. (1992). *The rediscovery of the mind*. Cambridge, MA: MIT Press.

Searle, J. R. (1995). *The construction of social reality*. London: Penguin.

Searle, J. R. (2010). *Making the social world: The structure of human civilization*. Oxford: Oxford University Press.

Searle, J. R. (2016). The limits of emergence: Reply to Tony Lawson. *Journal for the Theory of Social Behaviour, 46*(6), 400–412. doi:10.1111/jtsb.12125

von Bertalanffy, L. (1950). The theory of open systems in physics and biology. *Science, 111*(2872), 23–29. doi:10.1126/science.111.2872.23

von Bertalanffy, L. (2015). *General system theory: Foundations, development, applications* (Revised edition. ed.). New York: George Braziller, Inc.

Wight, C. (2016). Over socialising the social world(s)? *Journal for the Theory of Social Behaviour, 46*(4), 413–419. doi:10.1111/jtsb.12127

3 Social totalities and the nature of human communities

Social positioning theory provides an account of the constitution of social totalities. Therefore, central to an understanding of the theory is clarity regarding which totalities are classified as social. Identifying how the term social is used within social positioning theory is of particular importance because conceptions of social ontology are not all informed by the same understanding of which phenomena are appropriately classified as social.[1]

Moreover, it is common that conceptions of social ontology underemphasise the definition of social that informs their theories. Indeed, the term social is often defined either briefly or only in footnotes. If Lawson has regularly provided explicit definitions of social phenomena in his published work, these have never been developed in a sustained fashion. This has at times led to confusion and misunderstanding when other conceptions of social ontology have engaged with the Cambridge conception, and vice versa.[2]

To fully understand a conception of social ontology, one must be clear as to the phenomena covered by the account of social constitution it provides. Therefore, exploring how the term social is understood in some detail is not only worthwhile but necessary if one is to fully appreciate the explanatory power of social positioning theory. So, the aim of this chapter is to clearly outline how the term social is understood in social positioning theory and to indicate, consequently, which totalities are social.

I begin by analysing how Tony Lawson and the Cambridge group understand the term social, explaining how this definition has evolved over time. I then provide some examples, given the definition identified, of social totalities. Finally, I explain why, for Lawson, human communities are the most basic social totality and, as such, at this stage in the development of the theory, the constitution of such communities is the main focus of social positioning theory.

Defining social

The way the term social has been defined in Cambridge social ontology has evolved over time. In early work, Lawson (1994, p. 518) wrote that "criterial for the social [is] the property of depending upon human agency".

DOI: 10.4324/9781003110873-3

A decade later, Lawson (2003, p. 16) elaborated that "[b]y *social reality* or the social realm I mean that domain of all phenomena whose existence depends at least in part on us", specifying that the dependence on human beings needs only be *in part*.

A key addition to the definition then came through specifying that social phenomena are those "whose formation/coming into existence and/or continuing existence *necessarily* depend at least in part upon human beings and their interactions" (Lawson, 2015a, p. 21). This inclusion of the term *necessarily* was deemed essential as it "serves to exclude factors that in a sense depend on us but only contingently so, for example all the natural structures and life-forms that we could destroy but do not" (Lawson, 2015a, p. 48). So, for example, when the term *necessarily* is excluded, a tree could be interpreted as depending on us for its existence as we have the power to cut it down. But a tree, certainly one that is in the middle of a dense wild forest and unknown to anyone, is not a phenomenon that the Cambridge group considers should be categorised as social. So, the term *necessarily* serves to make clear that a phenomenon like a tree is not included by such a definition as social.

Then it was recognised that although the term *necessarily* helpfully excluded, from the definition of social, non-social phenomena that we have the power to destroy, there were other phenomena that continued to be included by such a definition that it was argued should not be considered social. Two key issues were raised. First, it was identified that the above definition did not make clear whether individual instances constituted by human beings of phenomena that can otherwise come into being without our involvement are social. In other words, is the individual instance of fire created by a human being a social phenomenon? Second, it was deemed necessary to further clarify how the term dependence was being used in this definition. Did dependence mean only that phenomena were brought into being by human beings? Did dependence also imply that such phenomena required continual reproduction by human beings to exist over time?

To address these issues and, as such, to further clarify the specific subset of phenomena referred to as social by the Cambridge group, Lawson, albeit in a footnote, provided the following definition:

> I take the social to be broadly those phenomena whose existence depends necessarily on us. More specifically, I take the social domain to be the set of instances of those (actual and possible) kinds of phenomena where, in the case of each such kind, the coming into being of all its instances necessitated/necessitates human beings and their interactions (so the social domain excludes all instances of those kinds, such as water, fire, or certain chemical compounds, where the coming into existence of only a subset of instances necessitated/necessitates human interaction). By a kind, here, I simply mean a grouping where the phenomena grouped share a set of non-accidental properties. The subset of social phenomena

in which I will be primarily interested in the current paper, which might be called the core social, comprise the instances of those social kinds where it is not only the case, re their instances, that their coming into being depends on human beings and their actions and interactions, but their continuing existence also does so. Possession of this later property could be built into the definition of the social. But that would seemingly result in the exclusion of specific kinds of human artefacts; at least this is so if a human artefact is understood as an item (intentionally) made by us, and if it is the case that there are kinds of human artefacts with instances that continue in existence without depending on us to do so (if there are none, the social simply reduces to the core social).

(Lawson, 2022, pp. 2–3)

While Lawson opens by retaining a definition in terms of those phenomena "whose existence depends necessarily on us", he adds several key points of clarification. The first addresses the question of whether an individual instance of fire produced by human beings should be classified as social? Lawson here further specifies that the word social should only be used to refer to those kinds of phenomena for which all instances depend necessarily on human beings for their existence.[3] As such, individual instances produced by human beings of kinds of phenomena that can otherwise come into being independently of human beings are not social. So, individual instances of fire produced by human beings are excluded from the definition as instances of fire can come into being in a manner that is independent of human beings.

The second clarification relates to how the term dependence is employed as part of this definition. Does dependence here only imply that the phenomenon could not have come into being without us? Or does it also mean that the phenomenon must be dependent on us over time, in the sense that its continuing existence is dependent on being reproduced through our actions? Here, Lawson draws a distinction between the core social and the social.[4] The core social includes those kinds of phenomena that depend on us for their existence in terms of both their coming into being and their continuing existence. But the social includes all those kinds of phenomena that depend on us for their coming into existence, regardless of whether or not their continuing existence depends on us. Therefore, even when a kind of phenomenon exists independently of us after it comes into being, it is social if every instance of that kind of phenomenon was constituted in a manner that depends necessarily on us.

Given these further clarifications, the definition of social that informs Cambridge social ontology can be summarised as follows. *A social phenomenon is any member of a kind whose every instance depends necessarily on us to come into being.* This includes a building that might be used as a house, which arguably continues to exist independently of us once we have built it, but not the fire in its fireplace. In so doing, Lawson demarcates social phenomena from all other phenomena, such as fire, which he refers to as non-social phenomena.[5]

The community as the most basic social totality

Social totalities, then, are those systems of components for which every instance of that kind of system depended necessarily on us to come into being. On that definition, there are numerous different types of social totalities, including "human communities, artefacts, language and communication systems" (Lawson, 2022, p. 1). Artefacts, for example, are phenomena constituted by us through the organisation of some set of physical, generally inanimate items.[6] As they are organised systems and depend on us for their coming into being, they are social totalities.[7]

Social positioning theory aims to account for the constitution of all of these different types of social totalities. That said, the theory has not yet been elaborated to the same extent in accounting for the constitution of each of these different types of social totality. Indeed, by some distance the human community is the social totality that has been the object of the most developed research. Why then, of all the different types of social totalities have communities come to occupy this privileged position in the development of the conception of social ontology defended in Cambridge? To answer this question, let us start by examining how Lawson conceptualises the community. For example, Lawson has written that a community is:

> [A]n identifiable, restricted, relatively enduring (if typically evolving) coherent grouping of people who share some set of (usually equally evolving) concerns. So conceived a specific community may or may not be regional, and where it is regional it can be pan-national or very highly localised or situated anywhere on a spectrum spanned by such cases. Different communities may, and clearly do, overlap, intersect and/or nest. We, each of us, interact with others within many different communities simultaneously.
>
> (Lawson, 2012, p. 359)

Lawson (2014, p. 7) has also identified the community as "any relationally organised social emergent or 'organisational form' that includes human beings amongst its components". Most recently, Lawson has characterised communities as:

> [T]hose social totalities that include human individuals, more specifically at least two individuals, among the elements relationally organised to form components. Human communities, so conceived, include families, neighbourhoods, schools, sports teams, corporations, rock bands, research groups, political parties, nations, international organisations, and so on.
>
> (Lawson, 2022, pp. 6–7)

So, if initially Lawson expressed his understanding of community in terms of a "coherent group of people" with shared concerns, over time it was specified that this coherence was precisely due to the fact that a community involved people organised to form components of a social totality. Communities are therefore distinct from other types of social totalities such as artefacts that do not include human beings among their components.

But understanding the nature of a community so conceived does not yet explain why communities and their constitution have become the focus of Lawson's conception of social ontology. Why then has the account of community constitution taken such a central place in Lawson's elaboration of social positioning theory? One reason that the centrality of community constitution was only recognised more recently could be that in earlier stages of the development of social positioning theory the principles associated with community constitution were thought to apply equally to other social totalities.[8] Another reason could be that Lawson now considers that other social totalities, such as artefacts, are comparatively easily accounted for:

> [I]f artefacts are the more common form of social totality, the manner of their organisation is, at an abstract level anyway, [. . .] fairly easy to grasp; the relational structure will usually take the form of a spatial arrangement of the elements involved, with the arrangement rendered fixed (where it is) by way of the employment of some bonding agents, such as glue, cement, screws and so on.
>
> (Lawson, 2022, p. 4)[9]

But, most importantly, it is that, for Lawson (2016b, p. 447), "the community, constituted through the organising of human beings amongst its components, is the most basic form of social totality". What does Lawson mean by most basic? Lawson argues:

> We are all born into some or other set of communities, and, in the modern world anyway, we interact as human beings only as participants in a number of communities; all coordinated human interactions take place in, and depend fundamentally upon the organising structures of, human communities.
>
> (Lawson, 2022, p. 7)

Therefore, given that all social phenomena depend necessarily on us to come into being and that we are all born into communities, all social phenomena must be constituted in a manner that is community relative. In other words, for Lawson:

> The community is the more fundamental sort [of social totality] not least in the sense that each of the [. . .] [other social totalities] presupposes the existence of human communities, each is community

relative, and, in most cases at least, each is constituted to be formed into a specific community component. So, communities are an essential condition for them all.

(Lawson, 2022, p. 4)

Communities are the most basic social totality in the sense that communities are presupposed by all other social totalities. If communities, like all other social totalities, depend on human beings, they do so differently in that human beings are among the elements organised as their components. All other social totalities then depend on human beings to bring them into being but not as their components. These other social totalities are constituted by human beings that are already always components of various communities and, as such, are community relative. So, the community can be conceived of as the central social totality.

That is not to say that the community is somehow at the foundation of social reality. Lawson (2012, p. 371) is adamant that "the community [. . .] is [. . .] not [. . .] a foundational category (there clearly are no social foundations)". Rather, we are all born into communities and as such community membership is a precondition for action. Communities, then, are constituted with human community participants among their components and, therefore, in turn, depend on us to exist. Community constitution is at the centre of all social constitution and, as such, the initial focus that has been placed on developing an account of community positioning has been warranted.

In short, communities are social totalities that include human persons among their components. Community positioning is the most developed aspect of positioning to date because communities are the most basic social totality. Communities are basic in the sense that all other social constitution takes place in a manner that is dependent on human beings that are all organised such that they give rise to components of communities. Therefore, all social constitution is community relative.

Concluding remarks

The purpose of this chapter has been to detail how Cambridge social ontology has defined the set of phenomena whose constitution are the focus of study of social positioning theory. This definition has rarely been examined or elaborated in any great detail. Yet for one to fully grasp the conception defended, it is essential to clearly understand the set of phenomena whose constitution the theory seeks to explain.

For Lawson and the Cambridge Social Ontology Group, those phenomena considered to be social are members of those kinds whose every instance depends necessarily on us for their existence. So a building that might be used as a house is a social phenomenon, but a fire, even one made by us, is not.

If the constitution of all social totalities, then, is the focus of social positioning theory, for Lawson, there is a social totality that is more basic or central than the others—the community. For Lawson, a community is a social totality that includes human beings among its components. It is basic in the sense that all social phenomena depend necessarily on human beings and all human beings are born into communities. Therefore, all social phenomena are constituted in a manner that is community relative.

Consequently, the focus of the development of social positioning theory has been to provide an account of community constitution. In the following chapters, the features of social positioning theory outlined and the principles examined are those of community social positioning. I turn now to the organising structure of such communities.

Notes

1 For example, the understanding of the term social that informs the work of John Searle differs from that which informs Lawson. A social phenomenon—or social fact—is, for Searle (2010, p. 156), "any fact that contains a collective intentionality of two or more human or animal agents". For Searle, collective intentionality is a capacity that we and animals share and, as such, social phenomena can be constituted by both human beings and other animals. So, for example, for Searle (2016, p. 401), "[m]y dog Tarski and I going for walk is a paradigm social fact". Searle would also consider the cooperative activities of groups of animals, such as when lions hunt in packs to constitute a social fact. This definition then also extends to cover all manner of cooperative activities engaged in by groups of human beings such as playing in a symphony. That said, although Searle defines social phenomena in terms of shared instances of collective intentionality, he is not actually very interested in explaining the constitution of the phenomena he defines as social. Rather, his focus in elaborating his conception of social ontology is not on social facts in general but on the "subclass of social facts" that he names institutional facts—those that are only constituted by human beings. Searle (2016, p. 401) does not focus on social facts in general as they "are much less interesting to analyze because they are rather boring in their logical structure". Indeed, on Searle's own definition, he is not proposing a conception of social ontology but rather of institutional ontology. He, by his own admission, finds the nature of social reality in general "rather boring". The interesting things, for Searle (2010, p. ix), are "nation-states, money, corporations, ski clubs, summer vacations, cocktail parties, and football games". Searle (2016, p. 401) only wants to analyse "the distinctive features of human social ontology".

2 Searle's definition of the social is clearly very different to Lawson's and consequently demarcates a different realm of phenomena. A pack of lions hunting would not, for example, for Lawson, constitute a social phenomenon. This difference, however, has not always been adequately recognised and has led to misunderstandings that, once the differences in definition are made explicit, can be easily resolved. Take, for example, an argument between Lawson and Searle as to the role of language in social constitution. Lawson (2016a, p. 360) has argued that "Searle puts his primary emphasis on language as a foundational feature of social reality". In other words, Lawson has claimed that Searle argues you need a language before you can have a social reality. For Lawson (2016a, p. 375), this cannot be the case as "it is difficult to imagine [. . .] how language could emerge outside of a community". Searle, however, does not

argue that language is necessary for the constitution of social reality in general. For Searle, a social fact is constituted when collective intentionality is shared by two or more human or animal agents. Animals other than humans do not have language, can share collective intentionality and, therefore, for Searle, social reality can be constituted without language. Moreover, Searle does not deny that a pre-existing social reality would be necessary for the development of language. Indeed, Searle (2010, p. 65) argues that "as far as we know there were early humans more or less like ourselves walking on the face of the earth without language, and later they got language". These humans, for Searle, had pre-linguistic forms of collective intentionality and therefore constituted social phenomena that pre-existed the development of language.

This misunderstanding arises due to Lawson inadequately appreciating the differences between his own understanding and the definition of social that underpins Searle's conception. While Searle does argue that language is necessary for *human social reality* and specifically the *institutional facts* that are distinct to human social reality, he does not argue that it is necessary for social reality in general. But for Lawson, human social reality and social reality are the same thing and, therefore, Lawson has understandably interpreted Searle as saying that language is necessary for social reality. This, however, is a mistake as human social reality is only a subset of the realm Searle demarcates as social reality.

But Lawson is not alone in inadequately appreciating that a different definition of social is informing his interlocutor. Searle has accused Lawson of inadequately identifying the difference between human and animal social ontology and the role of language in that difference. Searle (2016, p. 401) regularly argues that a "serious weakness" of Lawson's conception is that it "applies equally to humans and animals". And, for Searle (2016, p. 401), "[i]f an account does not distinguish between human social ontology and animal social ontology, it cannot answer the essential questions about human social life". Lawson, however, has in fact been quite clear that he considers language to be necessary for the constitution of complex social phenomena of the sort that Searle identifies when arguing for a distinction between human and animal social ontology such as, for example, a government. Indeed, Lawson (2016a, p. 377) clearly states, "I do not of course deny that very complex contemporary forms of social or 'institutional' reality involve a deontology that requires language as a necessary condition". Here, Searle misunderstands how Lawson understands the term social. For Lawson, there is no issue of distinction between human and animal social ontology as he defines social phenomena in terms of human beings. On Lawson's definition, there cannot be an animal social ontology. Searle's claim is, then, that Lawson does not recognise the role of language in the constitution of those phenomena that only human beings can constitute. But Lawson would simply interpret that same class of phenomena as complex social phenomena and makes clear that he recognises the important role of language in their constitution.

3 Lawson (2022, p. 3), by kind, means a grouping that shares "a set of non-accidental properties". Lawson does not specify the nature of the properties that need to be shared such that a set of phenomena constitute a kind as different types of similarities can mean that a set of phenomena belong to a kind. The phenomena that form a kind can, for example, share a relevant form of organisational structure. Or they may share a common function. Lawson has also at times used the terms kind and category interchangeably:

> In carving up the non-social realm, appropriately positioned human beings determine the basis of any particular *kind*. [. . .] Once kinds or categories have been determined, thereafter it is nature, as it were, that decides

which of the things or stuff around us qualify as tokens or "members". Thus if human beings decide that anything with a chemical composition of H2O is a given kind called water, then whether or not various phenomena around constitute examples of water is not a matter that depends on deliberations or assessments; a liquid on my colleague's desk, for example, is water (or not) independently of what I or others might speculate about its nature.

(Lawson, 2014, p. 8)

Categories, however, are somewhat distinct from kinds. Specifically, categorisation is a process that is conducted by us and is fallible. Lawson (2014, p. 8) describes the process of categorisation as aiming to "carve nature at its joints". By there being joints in nature, Lawson means that there are different kinds of phenomena whether we exist or not. But as we do not have direct access to those differences, in rendering those distinct kinds of phenomena intelligible to us, we need to go through a process of categorisation whereby we carve up nature. Now while this process is fallible, and there is "no unique way to do this", the aim is to try and carve at its joints (Lawson, 2014, p. 8). Therefore, it is possible that kinds and categories may be different.

4 Lawson introduced such a distinction between the core social and the social as early as 2009. In an early draft of Lawson (2015a), he writes:

By the social realm is meant those phenomena, existents, properties, processes, structures and events whose coming into existence depends at least in part upon us, including most centrally those phenomena and features, etc., whose continuing existence depends on us. The latter continually dependent subset might collectively be said to constitute the core social realm.

This distinction, however, was not retained in the final published version of that paper and was not emphasised elsewhere by Lawson in print until Lawson (2022). Clive Lawson has also drawn on this distinction between social and core social, writing:

We can define "the social" as the domain that necessarily depends for its existence upon the activities of human beings. Thus a range of phenomena can be considered to be social, ranging from language and dance to tables and chairs. But my focus initially will be on those phenomena sometimes called core-social or cultural that have a mode of existence that depends entirely upon the ongoing activity of human beings. In other words, whilst tables or chairs come into existence only because of the activities of human beings, they then continue to exist largely independently of social activity—their mode of existence for the most part is independent of human activity. Other phenomena, such as language, norms of politeness, the highway code, credit, etc., exist primarily through being continually reproduced and transformed in and through the daily activities of human beings. Thus their mode of existence is, for the most part, dependent upon social activity, and so such phenomena are a core feature of social reality.

(C. Lawson, 2017, p. 39)

5 Whilst Lawson has not explicitly provided a definition of non-social phenomena, one can be derived, as follows, from the definition of social provided earlier. *A non-social phenomenon is any member of a kind for which at least one instance of the kind came into being independently of us.*

6 Lawson has often drawn on artefacts as examples to illustrate aspects of social positioning theory but has never explicitly outlined how he defines artefacts. Lawson (2015b, p. 221), however, has explained that artefacts

consist "of organisations of physical components, with the latter components themselves constituted as organisations of elements that pre-existed them etc." Or, in other words, "artefacts [. . .] do not have humans as components; rather they mostly [. . .] are constituted through the relational organisation of other artefacts" (Lawson, 2016a, p. 364). Moreover, he has added that "all artefacts [. . .] require the input of external human beings" (Lawson, 2016c, p. 432). It is also important to recognise that Lawson's understanding has been strongly influenced by the work of Clive Lawson. For Clive Lawson, the:

> [R]eason for using the term "artefact" rather than "object" is simply to signal that I am most concerned [. . .] with things that have been transformed to some degree by human activity. The term artefact literally means to make by art, and for this reason users of the term artefact are typically emphasising the importance of makers in the coming into being of some object. My emphasis is especially upon the idea that things have been reorganised or reconfigured.
> (C. Lawson, 2017, p. 63)

7 If artefacts are clearly social in the sense of depending on us for their coming into being, not all artefacts form part of what Lawson has referred to as the core social. Clive Lawson has illustrated that:

> [A]rtefacts [. . .] depend on human action, but depend on it in a variety of different, and apparently contradictory, ways. On the one hand, artefacts can be assembled, fashioned or modified by human action but continue to exist whether or not they continue to be acted upon by human beings; material artefacts such as hammers, paintings, houses, etc., once constructed, become relatively enduring independently of human action that brought them into being. On the other hand, such objects would not be "hammers", "paintings", "houses", etc., if human beings suddenly ceased to exist. Pinning down the sociality of artefacts amounts to explaining these two apparently conflictual statements, that artefacts, once made, are both independent of and dependent upon human activities.
> (C. Lawson, 2017, p. 73)

Clive Lawson goes on to argue:

> [T]he sociality of artefacts comes, apart from the obvious sense in which they are constructed by human beings, from their being positioned, where the positions involved are reproduced and transformed through human practices. The sociality of artefacts then refers to those characteristics and features an artefact possesses in virtue of the way that it is positioned. For some artefacts, such features may be all important. For example, it is only because of the collective agreement that exists about cash or passports that they can be used in the ways that they are. For other artefacts, such as hammers and engines, positionality is only really responsible for their continued existence qua hammer and engine. Their continued use in practice serves only to maintain or reproduce their identities or the ways in which they are normally used. Their ability to perform a particular task, or to be used in particular ways, remains unaffected.
> (C. Lawson, 2017, p. 75)

8 As I explain in Chapter 4, the organising structure of human communities is made up of relations in the form of rights and obligations. Lawson, in earlier stages of the development of social positioning theory, at times seemingly

indicated that relations in the form of rights and obligations were involved in the constitution of all social totalities, including artefactual totalities:

> Even in the case where individual things and artefacts are incorporated as components of other artefacts—where, as noted, mere placement may be sufficient for an appropriate physical orientation—the ability of the items *qua* components and so of their embedding totalities to "function" in practice ultimately rests on (often informal) more general rights and obligations that pervade the wider community and accompany their constitution. Most obviously, it is essential that the components not be removed from the totality in which they are incorporated, or broken or otherwise tampered with. Though often taken for granted where it prevails, a situation where all community participants recognise obligations not so to tamper is an achievement. The fact that unauthorised removal or destruction of such items, if or where it occurs, is in very many communities treated as a criminal act only reinforces this point. Ultimately, the functioning of social reality everywhere is subject to the influence of rights and obligations that are part and parcel of processes of social positioning.
>
> (Lawson, 2019, pp. 14–15)

Lawson no longer considers rights and obligations to be involved in the constitution of all social totalities.

9 Lawson has also referred to the organisation of artefacts as the "simplest" form of social positioning:

> [W]hen an object is simply physically incorporated as a component (*not* of a community directly, but) of an artefact—as with inserting a pane of glass in a space for a window in a wall of house, or a wooden block in a space for a door of the same house—the "opening" created is typically so oriented physically that the mere placement of an appropriate object within it ensures that relevant capacities possessed can be drawn on. This is the simplest case of social positioning [. . .].
>
> (Lawson, 2019, p. 13)

It is possible to readily appreciate what Lawson means when he says that this is the "simplest" case of social positioning. It is very easy to picture positioning in terms of a pane of glass filling a hole in a wall or a wooden block filling a space for a door. In that sense it is simple.

References

Lawson, C. (2017). *Technology and isolation*. Cambridge: Cambridge University Press.

Lawson, T. (1994). The nature of Post Keynesianism and its links to other traditions: A realist perspective. *Journal of Post Keynesian Economics, 16*(4), 503–538.

Lawson, T. (2003). *Reorienting economics*. London and New York: Routledge.

Lawson, T. (2012). Ontology and the study of social reality: Emergence, organisation, community, power, social relations, corporations, artefacts and money. *Cambridge Journal of Economics, 36*(2), 345–385. doi:10.1093/cje/ber050

Lawson, T. (2014). The nature of the firm and peculiarities of the corporation. *Cambridge Journal of Economics, 39*(1), 1–32. doi:10.1093/cje/beu046

Lawson, T. (2015a). A conception of social ontology. In S. Pratten (Ed.), *Social ontology and modern economics* (pp. 19–52). London and New York: Routledge.

Lawson, T. (2015b). The modern corporation: The site of a mechanism (of global social change) that is out-of-control? In M. S. Archer (Ed.), *Generative mechanisms transforming the social order* (pp. 205–231). Dordrecht: Springer.

Lawson, T. (2016a). Comparing conceptions of social ontology: Emergent social entities and/or institutional facts? *Journal for the Theory of Social Behaviour, 46*(4), 359–399. Doi:10.1111/jtsb.12126

Lawson, T. (2016b). Ontology and social relations: Reply to Doug Porpora and to Colin Wight. *Journal for the Theory of Social Behaviour, 46*(4), 438–449. Doi:10.1111/jtsb.12128

Lawson, T. (2016c). Some critical issues in social ontology: Reply to John Searle. *Journal for the Theory of Social Behaviour, 46*(4), 426–437.

Lawson, T. (2019). *The nature of social reality: Issues in social ontology*. London and New York: Routledge.

Lawson, T. (2022). Social positioning theory. *Cambridge Journal of Economics, 46*(1), 1–39. doi:10.1093/cje/beab040

Searle, J. R. (2010). *Making the social world: The structure of human civilization*. Oxford: Oxford University Press.

Searle, J. R. (2016). The limits of emergence: Reply to Tony Lawson. *Journal for the Theory of Social Behaviour, 46*(6), 400–412. doi:10.1111/jtsb.12125

4 Social positions and community organising structure

Social positions are the organising structure of social totalities. Lawson (2022, p. 5) explains that the term position—whether referring to a social phenomenon or otherwise—is "mostly used to express a relational phenomenon" existing in reference to some whole or totality and "has the connotation of something that can become occupied (or entered into)".[1] Therefore, in general terms, a social position is a relational phenomenon, which exists as part of a social totality, that can be occupied:

> Clearly, if position is an appropriate term to employ for any relationally determined site or location of component formation, whatever the totality, then it is equally apt that in social positioning theory the label social position is used for any such location within a social totality, including within human artefacts, languages, and so on.
>
> (Lawson, 2022, p. 6)[2]

If all positions are relationally determined, the nature of these relations varies between different types of social totalities. In some, such as artefacts, the relations may primarily be spatial, with bonding occurring via the use of adhesives of some sort.[3] Others such as languages are yet to be examined in any great detail from the perspective of social positioning theory and warrant further research.

The aim, in this chapter, is to examine the nature of the relations that constitute the organising structure of human communities. In communities, social positions are packages or sets of rights and obligations. I begin by outlining the key features of social positions in the form of rights and obligations and consider how such positions might emerge. Key, then, to the continued existence of such a structure is that the rights and obligations are collectively accepted. I explain how Lawson understands the notion of collective acceptance before, finally, showing that community organising structure so constituted must be underpinned by trust.

DOI: 10.4324/9781003110873-4

Rights and obligations

In communities, social positions are packages or sets of rights and obligations.[4] These rights and obligations form a relational structure in the sense that each right/obligation that figures in the constitution of one position is matched to an obligation/right that figures in the constitution of typically, although not necessarily, a different position.[5] In other words:

> [T]he rights associated with any particular position [. . .] are always internally or constitutively related to obligations attached to certain, usually different, positions and their occupants. These matched rights and obligations thereby constitute a fundamental form of social relation [. . .].[6]
>
> (Lawson, 2019, p. 15)

Due to the obligatory component of such matched pairs of rights and obligations, social relations of this form are necessarily power relations. Indeed, for Lawson (2016c, p. 439), "the feature of conferring 'power over' is [. . .] the very essence of a right-obligation positional relationship". Relations in the form of rights and obligations involve power because where a position occupant has a right that corresponds to an obligation of another position occupant, the former has power over the latter. In other words:

> They work as power relations in that the exercising of a position right by one party leads to another, with a corresponding or matched obligation, doing what is requested or expected, even if the latter party feels it is the last thing he or she wants to do.
>
> (Lawson, 2019, p. 15)

As such, "matched rights and obligations can be thought of, respectively, as positive and negative (deontic) powers" (Lawson, 2022, p. 11).[7]

Community social positions can be broadly divided into two different types, person positions and non-person positions. Person positions are packages of rights and obligations that "stipulate allowed and required ways of acting for any party associated with the position" (Lawson, 2022, p. 10). Non-person positions are subsets of the rights and obligations of person positions that "stipulate allowed and required uses (or ways of being employed or operated, etc.) of any party associated with the non-person [. . .] position" (Lawson, 2022, p. 10). Therefore, community organising structure is primarily made up of person positions. In other words, the total number of rights and obligations included in a particular community are exhausted by the rights and obligations of the total number of person positions. The rights and obligations that identify non-person positions are subsets of the rights and obligations of the community person positions with those rights and obligations always exercised and accessed by the occupants of person positions.

How, then, are rights and obligations elaborated? Broadly speaking, this occurs in two ways:

> The rights and obligations constituting positions may result from (though without necessarily being entirely in conformity with) authoritative declarations (usually expressed in the form of codifications [of those rights and obligations that are desired by the authority]). They may also (and likely do more typically) emerge spontaneously through general human interaction, with rights being implicit in certain widely followed individual actions and with obligations manifest as norms of human activity.
>
> (Lawson, 2022, p. 11)

The first is a planned process in which rights and obligations are formally outlined or declared. The second is a more informal process in which rights and obligations develop through actions becoming routinised over time. For Lawson, the more formal process occurs when rights and obligations:

> [E]merge via processes of negotiation whereby official agreements are reached and the content [. . .] (regarding allowed and required ways of doing things for those appropriately positioned) are recorded in some manner, in signed documents, such as contracts and deeds of ownership, etc.
>
> (Lawson, 2016b, p. 366)

Take, for example, a lectureship being made available at a university. Here, perhaps a staffing committee and other relevant members of a department may identify the need for a new lecturer and may make a request to a faculty or wider university for funding for such a post and eventually the creation of a lectureship might be approved. The relevant members of the department will then elaborate a set of required and permitted ways of going on—often then written down as part of a job pack—that the potential lecturer will be subjected to should they be appointed. A lecturer, for example, "is typically allowed to use a faculty library or work in her/his faculty office at any time of the day" and is "typically not only allowed but additionally required to give lectures, and set and mark examinations, etc." (Lawson, 2012, p. 367). These ways of going on are then grounded in the actual actions of the appointed lecturer.

Alternatively, Lawson has described how rights and obligations can emerge in a more spontaneous manner as follows:

> Many of the more interesting sets of rights and obligations, or forms of behaviour that are taken to represent the content of community

agreement or acceptance, emerge in a somewhat more spontaneous manner and are manifest in the structuring of community collective practices, practices that are thereafter taken as constituting the accepted ways of doing things in the respective community. Obvious examples are numerous forms of queuing, perhaps in regards to food (say at rock concerts) or for entrance/access to roads in heavy traffic, and so on.

(Lawson, 2016b, p. 367)

Lawson (2016d, p. 964) also provides an example where "an emergent protesting group may quite spontaneously position and rally behind say a (perhaps even somewhat reluctant) leader or spokesperson". For Lawson, it is through such informal and spontaneous kinds of processes that rights and obligations would have emerged prior to the existence of language[8]:

[I]t is easy enough to imagine of early hominids that where experimental cooperative practices are discovered to be advantageous in some way they might be repeated by the discoverers and imitated by others, perhaps even to a point where dispositions so to act are established. It is also easy to imagine how certain new sets of cooperative practices might link or fit with those already repeatedly followed, so that their success is linked to those already in place. It is equally easily imaginable that new arrivals on the scene including children come to believe that in the relevant context the practices in question are the done way, the natural or given way. In consequence, in seeking to fit in, to conform, to belong, they find reason to pursue goals in ways, or according to practices, they otherwise might not have been inclined to follow. In other words, it is imaginable how deontology could have emerged without language.

(Lawson, 2016b, p. 374)[9]

So, rights and obligations can emerge with the routinised human actions that develop within communities.[10] The expectation that a particular way of proceeding will be followed by members of a community is sufficient for it to be appropriate to speak of there being an obligation.[11] Moreover, even when rights and obligations emerge through some declarative process, they are always grounded in human actions. Therefore, the conception that Lawson (2016b, p. 367) defends "is of a social reality that is mind-dependent but not mind determined; there is always a practical dimension".[12]

Collective acceptance

Once elaborated, rights and obligations—community social positions— must be collectively accepted. Indeed, for Lawson (2019, p. 16), "social reality is seen to depend fundamentally on the generalised acceptance, throughout specific communities, of structures of (community-specific and positional) social relations (matched pairs of rights and obligations)". So, community constitution requires human beings qua community members to collectively accept matching sets of rights and obligations:

> How precisely [. . .] does social binding occur according to this frame-work, so constituting communities as organised systems or totalities? It does so precisely through a generalised acceptance of the range of position rights and obligations just noted.
>
> (Lawson, 2019, p. 15)

But what does acceptance mean here? For Lawson (2012, p. 360), "the category of acceptance here has nothing to do with preference, agreement, support or approval, etc.". Rather, for Lawson:

> [T]he term indicates a way of proceeding that is in fact widely ad-hered to or observed or recognised by members of a specific com-munity, whatever its intrinsic appeal. As such the term acceptance here, a form of collective or community acceptance (in contrast to the more evaluative notion of individual acceptance that I consider in due course), is effectively a status. It carries, and rests upon, community-wide recognition and serves to constitute a way of proceeding as the done way.
>
> (Lawson, 2012, p. 360)[13]

Lawson has also, more recently, formulated his understanding of collective, or community participant, acceptance as follows:

> This is "acceptance" in the sense of a widespread *going along with*, at least for the time being. Such acceptance does *not* necessitate wide-spread participant agreement, liking, or any other positive orientation [. . .], and may indeed be mostly grudging.
>
> (Lawson, 2022, p. 9)

The issue that Lawson faces is that the term acceptance does, at least for some, carry connotations of approval and therefore is problematic, given the meaning that he is trying to convey. In other conceptions of social ontol-ogy, this issue has been resolved by replacing the term acceptance with rec-ognition.[14] But if, for Lawson, collective acceptance can, and perhaps often does, involve something like collective recognition, it also involves rights and obligations being widely adhered to in the sense that they are gone along with. As with Lawson's conception of rights and obligations, collec-tive acceptance is also grounded in human action. So, collective recognition does not solve the problem and although something like collective "going along with" would more accurately describe the phenomenon Lawson is referring to, it seems a rather clumsy way of putting things. Therefore, until a better option is provided, collective acceptance—so defined—is retained.

Trust

A final key feature of Lawson's conception of rights and obligations is that he argues that such relations must be underpinned by trust[15]:

> [T]he efficacy of any structure of matched rights/obligations relations to the coordination and functioning of any social totality/community depends upon [. . .] the requirements that positioned occupants are not only aware of their obligations but also, and in particular, committed to meeting their positional obligations (whether highly specific to an individual or general, explicit or implicit, codified or whatever), and prepared to trust that others will meet their own. Trust and trustworthiness together are, I believe, reasonably thought of as the glue of social communities. They are generally basic to everything we do as community participants, but are nowhere more fundamental, I suggest, than to our meeting the obligations that derive from positions that we each and all multiply occupy.
>
> (Lawson, 2019, p. 16)[16]

For something that Lawson considers central to his conception, he has written a relatively small amount on the topic when elaborating social positioning theory. Rather, his views are scattered throughout earlier papers dealing with different topics:

> Despite the importance that Lawson assigns to trust, it remains a relatively under- theorised category within his framework [. . .]. Trust is rarely Lawson's primary focus—rather, he comments on it as he addresses other issues and topics.
>
> (Pratten, 2017, p. 1420)

Another member of the Cambridge Social Ontology Group, Stephen Pratten, therefore, has sought to go further in understanding Lawson's conception of trust. In particular, he has provided some suggestions as to how the idea that trust is a basic capacity that all human beings have might be developed. He observes that, in the way Lawson writes of trust, it appears as a primitive capacity that we all have:

> Trust for Lawson seems to operate as a primary attitude or background expectation that does not itself require prior justification. [. . .] Lawson sees trust as a primitive orientation to other community participants where it is expected, or taken for granted, that they will perform their part in co-operative activities.
>
> (Pratten, 2017, p. 1425)

However, that is not to say that this is some inherent capacity that we all have at birth. Rather, Pratten shows that Lawson conceives of trust as being a developmental response to the vulnerability into which we are all born:

> For Lawson trust seems to be fundamentally linked to our nature as dependent or vulnerable beings. [. . .] We are intrinsically vulnerable with our ordinary lives in society exposing us to the will of others with whom, typically, our connection is unchosen. Our extensive dependence on unchosen relations to others begins with infancy and childhood, and continues throughout life. Trust, on Lawson's account, is an attitude or orientation that anticipates that the other will have and display goodwill or solidarity toward me under conditions in which I am dependent or vulnerable. We cannot avoid being intrinsically dependent on others, but trust allows us to make an accommodation with this dependence and cooperate nonetheless.
>
> (Pratten, 2017, p. 1427)

Lawson argues that because, as infants, we are dependent on others for our survival, the relationships we develop with our caregivers necessarily involve the development of trust. Pratten goes further than Lawson and provides an account of the process through which trust develops from such relationships:

> Lawson points to the circumstances where infants remain profoundly dependent on their immediate caregivers—were it not for the cooperation of these caregivers, they would simply not survive. It is their extensive dependence that requires infants to affectively assume and anticipate that they will be cared for and that their needs will be attended to. In due course they come to feel the weight and steadiness of the concern of their immediate caregivers.
>
> (Pratten, 2017, p. 1429)

Lawson, seemingly, would refer to the relationship of dependence as trust. Pratten however, argues that this is perhaps more usefully understood as a precursor to the development of trust:

> Rather than infants learning to trust their primary caregivers, it may be better to characterise them as learning a fundamental antecedent to trust—namely, they develop a sense of their own self-worth and value. Infants in being able to count on their needs being met and the continuing attention of their caregivers and in thus feeling cared for gradually appreciate that they matter and are of value. [. . .] The establishment of routines whereby expectations are developed and then continually met engender a sense of being of worth or mattering, which is in turn reinforced by those routines being maintained.

Interactions between infant and primary caregivers establish for the infant its standing as being intrinsically valuable, as the treatment received from sufficiently attentive caregivers is internalised. Trust, or a sense of trust, can then be seen as emerging through a developmental sequence.

(Pratten, 2017, pp. 1429–1430)[17]

This account makes clear the sense in which trust can be understood as a basic feature of human development and interaction. Indeed, I do not question the account, given that something like trust necessarily develops through the caring relationships that we require to survive. But what is its relationship to rights and obligations?

Community organising structure in the form of packages or sets of rights and obligations that are always matched is a normative and not a deterministic order. As such, community components are not forced to comply with the rights and obligations of their positions and may choose to act otherwise. So, when Lawson speaks of being trustworthy, it is the characteristic of following through with the obligations associated with one's position. Trust, then, for Lawson, plays the role both of expecting that one's rights will be matched by another carrying out the corresponding obligation as well as committing oneself to carrying out one's own obligations. Trust, insofar as it relates to community constitution, is that capacity that guarantees reciprocity. In that sense, one can understand how it contributes to binding the organisational structure of rights and obligations together.

Concluding remarks

In social positioning theory, the organisational structure of social totalities is made up of social positions. The nature of the relations that constitute these positions differs between different kinds of social totalities. In human communities, these positions are relations in the form of matched packages or sets of rights and obligations. These rights and obligations can be elaborated, broadly speaking, in two different ways.

The first involves some formal declarative process that will often involve some sort of codification. The second is more spontaneous whereby rights and obligations emerge through various actions becoming routinised and as such expected of different members of the community. These rights and obligations must then be collectively accepted by community members. By collective acceptance, Lawson means a collective "going along with". As such, Lawson's account of rights and obligations and his understanding of collective acceptance are expressed in terms of the ways in which community members proceed. These phenomena are, for Lawson, grounded in the actions of human beings.

But if an understanding of community organising structure in the form of social positions is a central feature of social positioning theory, we do not yet have a complete account of community constitution. For to constitute a community, items—including people, things and even other whole subcommunities—must be allocated to positions and so organised by relations in the form of rights and obligations. Therefore, I turn now to the processes involved in allocating items to community social positions and the resulting formation of community components.

Notes

1 Lawson (2022, p. 5) provides examples such as "on the map of the UK in front of me, a symbol representing the city of Edinburgh is conventionally described as positioned (as occupying a position) towards the top; and the symbol for Southampton is described as positioned (occupying a position) towards the bottom" as well as "Y may take a position to the left of that of an opponent in a political debate or be positioned on the left of the Party".

2 Lawson acknowledges that some may prefer to employ alternative expressions to social position, particularly when referring to the positioning of people, such as roles. Lawson explains why he favours the term position in the following passage by comparing it to Margaret Archer's use of the term role:

> I am aware that where I use the category *social position* that of *social role* is employed by some and notably by Margaret Archer. Although there is seemingly little disagreement over the nature of the features of social reality that the competing terms are used to designate, I stick with the term social position, not just (and not least) because this is the terminology I have adopted throughout my contributions, but also because, on balance, I continue to think it the more appropriate. In the text I shall argue that associated with (the status that I am calling) social position are sets of rights and obligations. Archer's reason for preferring the category role is that she associates the term position with various groupings such as the downtrodden or poor or homeless or nouveaux riches where the individuals included are not the bearers of any associated rights and obligations. These, Archer argues, are heterogeneous categories that do not correspond to social identities, as outlined above. I agree that the downtrodden, the poor, the homeless as well as nouveaux riches are not the sorts of categories that indicate social status of a sort that carries associated rights and responsibilities (though heterogeneity itself is not a problem *per se*; there are many types of UK citizen but still UK citizenship brings [positional] rights and obligations). But I would not refer to these sorts of categories (poor, downtrodden, homeless, etc) as social positions either. For sure, in describing an individual as, say, poor one might interpret this statement as meaning that the income of the individual is associated with a "position" (or more likely a range of positions), on some considered- to-be relevant income distribution, and so on. But here the word position has a different meaning, and referring to being poor as a position is really an imprecise short hand. Role too can be given different, including loose, meanings as in "accepting to take on the role of X (or even a poor person) in some play"; or "acknowledging that everyone at the football club played some role in the team's defeat and relegation"; or X likes to act the role of a fool. The reason I prefer the term position on balance is that it has the connotation of existing beyond simply individual choice, being ultimately a community property.

In all cases, even in the loose usages just discussed, we speak easily of individuals *taking on* roles, whereas individuals are more often said to be *allocated to*, placed in, or finding themselves in, positions. Although, individuals may indeed choose to apply for, or work to achieve, certain positions, most cannot be taken on just like that, whereas roles, it seems to me, do very often carry this individualistic connotation, and for that reason does seem to me to express far more subjective and temporary designations. Ultimately of course the meaning will be clear from, and perhaps determined only in, context. Anyway readers should be aware that the category social position as utilised here is much the same as social role as employed by Archer and others.

(Lawson, 2014c, p. 29)

Authors such as Dewey have also employed the term office. Pratten has argued that Dewey's use of the term office is very similar to Lawson's use of the term position:

The terms office and position may for many carry similar immediate connotations but the correspondences between this aspect of Dewey's social ontology and social positioning theory are a good deal more extensive and substantial than this. Both approaches maintain that human beings are not intrinsically persons but rather that certain individuals and groups of individuals come to occupy the office of person or position of legal person. For Dewey and social positioning theory individuals in coming to occupy an office or being positioned are thereby enmeshed in configurations of social relations involving paired sets of matching rights and obligations or duties. Dewey argues that the traits of the individual as a human being and those that arise from holding an office are distinct, social positioning theory distinguishes the relational properties possessed by positioned items from the properties of the items positioned. According to Dewey central to the establishment of an office is widespread habitual compliance with group requirements, for social positioning theory community participant collective acceptance grounds community social constitution. Neither Dewey nor social positioning theory conceives of there being a unique, or privileged, way in which offices or positions are established—they are understood as emerging from various types of process. Both perspectives see things as well as individuals as being capable of coming to occupy offices or positions, albeit with individuals occupying offices/positions in a distinctive manner. In recognizing that things come to occupy offices Dewey is concerned to emphasize the importance of distinguishing within the appearing object between itself in its "primary qualities" and itself in its "signifying office", in social positioning theory the positioning of things implies they, as components of embedding totalities, are never reducible to the things that become relationally organized in forming the components.

(Pratten, 2022, pp. 289–290)

3   Lawson refers to these positions as (artefactual) object or non-person positions. Indeed, Lawson (2022, p. 10) explains that he uses "the category object position elsewhere also to cover those sites or social positions where items are positioned to form parts or components of artefacts". These (artefactual) object positions are generally opened through making physical space into which inanimate objects and often other artefacts are allocated and so formed into (artefactual) non-person components. These components are then held together physically. Clive Lawson, on the other hand, often uses the term "recombination" for the process through which artefacts become components of other artefacts and then

reserves "positioning" for the process through which the artefact is incorporated as a component of a community. Authors such as Searle have argued that the term position always indicates a spatial phenomenon but Lawson has made clear that:

> I do not [. . .] accept Searle's supposed literal interpretation of position as spatial location. The (Latin and French) etymology of the term associates the term with (amongst other things) placement and arrangement but not necessarily with spatial features. The latter is but a special case.
>
> (Lawson, 2016e, p. 436)

4 The manner in which Lawson conceptualises rights and obligations is distinct from ostensibly associated notions—often presented under the headings of deontology or deontic powers—mobilised in approaches to social ontology influenced by analytic philosophy. The central influence for such approaches is John Searle. For Searle (2010, pp. 8–9), deontic powers are "rights, duties, obligations, requirements, permissions, authorizations, entitlements, and so on". These powers, for Searle, are key to understanding human society as they serve the purpose of providing motivations for acting that are over and above our desires, a feature that serves to distinguish human societies from those of animals. Searle argues that it is precisely the existence of such motivations that holds human societies together. Indeed, for Searle (2015, p. 508), "deontic powers [. . .] are the glue that holds human civilization together because they provide us with reasons for action that are independent of our desires". Searle's conception of deontology is inextricably bound up with language. Indeed, he argues both that deontology is an inescapable feature of language and that deontology requires language. Lawson's conception of rights and obligations does not consider language to be an essential requirement for deontology. I provide further context in relation to these differences in later footnotes.

5 Lawson provides an example to illustrate such a situation where the:

> [R]ights of the employer to stipulate that employees turn up at a workplace by a given time and carry out various tasks are matched to obligations of various employees to be in the workplace by the given time, and to undertake the various tasks in question. Similarly, the right of employees to remuneration for having conformed to these obligations is matched to an obligation of the employer to pay. The right of students to attend lectures is matched to obligations of lecturers to prepare and deliver them; the right that lecturers and students each have to request books in a faculty library is matched to obligations of librarians to fetch them (if stored away somewhere) and sign them out; and so on.
>
> (Lawson, 2019, p. 15)

6 Lawson is, however, careful to note that rights and obligations are not the only form of social relation:

> The contention I do maintain is not that the scope of social reality reduces to positions, rights and obligations, nor that relations of matching rights and obligations are the only kind to be found in the social realm [. . .], but rather that a case can be made for regarding them as being, from a social ontological perspective, a fundamental, and perhaps the most fundamental, form of relation. For they are distinguished in being essential to the constitution of social reality, working at all levels to sustain a degree of continuity and stability despite social reality being everywhere processual in nature.
>
> (Lawson, 2016c, p. 447)

That said, I acknowledge that there are times in which Lawson has made statements that could be reasonably interpreted as implying that matched pairs of rights and obligations are the only form of social relation. For example, Lawson (2012, p. 368) writes that "a social relation is just (or is first and foremost) an accepted set of rights and obligations holding between, and connecting, two or more positions or occupants of positions". In addition, Lawson (2016b, p. 365) has stated that "rights and obligations are indeed positive and negative powers, and so all social relations are power relations". Despite such passages, Lawson has been very clear in recent publications that his view is that rights and obligations are not the only form of social relation.

7 Lawson uses the terms deontology and deontic powers interchangeably with rights and obligations. I acknowledge that the term deontology is also used to refer to a position in ethical theory but any use of the term in this chapter is not associated with such perspectives.

8 The context in which Lawson developed this argument was in response to Searle's claim that you cannot have deontology without language. For Searle (2016, p. 409), "all deontology requires some form of linguistic representation". The reason for this is that, for Searle, there is a particular form of commitment that is inherent to speech acts. And it is only this particular form of commitment that, in Searle's view, brings with it deontology. To illustrate this point, Searle (2010, p. 65) draws a contrast with an imagined "race of early humans possessing the biological forms of intentionality, both individual and collective, but lacking language" who "are capable of cooperative behavior and [. . .] have the full range of perception, memory, belief, desire, prior intentions, and intentions-in-action". Searle argues that although pre-linguistic intentional states such as belief or desire do in some sense commit a person, they do not do so in a manner that constitutes deontic powers such as he conceives them in relation to the constitution of institutional facts. Searle (2010, p. 87) argues that "a belief is a commitment to truth and a desire is a commitment to satisfaction" but sees such commitments as being quite different to those made through the use of speech acts.

To illustrate this, Searle compares a belief and a statement made about that same belief:

> Both the belief and the corresponding statement involve commitments. But the commitment of the statement is much stronger. If the privately held belief turns out to be false I need only revise it. But in the case of the statement, I am committed not only to revision in the case of falsehood, but I am committed to being able to provide reasons for the original statement, I am committed to sincerity in making it, and I can be held publicly responsible if it turns out to be false.
>
> (Searle, 2010, p. 82)

While Searle (2010, pp. 81–82) defines commitment as involving two parts, "first, the notion of an undertaking that is hard to reverse and, second, the notion of an obligation", it does seem that in his view it is only commitment "in the full public sense that combines irreversibility and obligation", by which he means commitments made through speech acts. Therefore, it is only, in Searle's terms, when a responsibility is recognised via a public or social form of commitment, which he argues is only possible through language, that you truly have deontology. Indeed, Searle (2010, p. 82) states clearly that "in the full sense that involves the public assumption of irreversible obligations, there is no such deontology without language". In other words, to have deontology "in the full sense" the commitments must be made to other people who will hold you to them. And, for Searle, this can only be done through language. This argument is, of course, bound up with Searle's extensive work on language. For more on his account of language, see, for example, Searle (1969, 1979, 1983, 1992, 1995, 2001, 2002, 2010).

9　In this explanation of the emergence of deontology in groups of early hominids, Lawson draws on the terminology of collective practice. Lawson no longer regularly employs this terminology. In the first chapter of Lawson (2019), for example, there is no mention of collective practice. In Lawson (2022), it is mentioned once. The reason that Lawson no longer regularly employs the terminology of collective practice is because the terms rights and obligations are able to describe the same phenomena that Lawson previously referred to using the term collective practice. So, in earlier work, Lawson (2013, p. 82), for example, argued that in "the social realm, specifically, the organisational structure takes the form of community-accepted collective practices with their (often implicit) sets of rights and obligations, and so forth". Collective practices, in such passages, are presented as a central component of the organisation of social totalities. But in more recent accounts—namely those in which the importance of social positioning has been more fully recognised—Lawson identifies that the organisational relational structure of social totalities is made up of positions and their matching rights and obligations. What, then, has changed? The answer is that the focus in recent years on developing, and formalising the basic principles of, social positioning theory has led to both a greater recognition of the scope of certain categories as well as an emphasis on analytical clarity. In that context, Lawson has found that the phenomena previously referred to in terms of collective practice can be more usefully referred to in terms of rights and obligations. How can that be?

Consider how Lawson defines collective practice:

> By a *collective practice* I mean a specific way of going on that: (i) is recognised, over an interval in time and within some specific community, as the accepted way of proceeding with regard to achieving a particular outcome; (ii) involves the participation of all members of the community, either through their direct adherence to the given accepted way of proceeding, or through their acting in other ways that facilitate, presuppose or otherwise maintain the latter, including avoiding intentionally impeding the actions of those more directly participating.
>
> (Lawson, 2012, p. 360)

Lawson uses the term collective practice to refer to the collectively accepted ways of going on within a community, which involve permitted and required actions on behalf of community members. Lawson conceptualises rights and obligations in the same way, these being collectively accepted, permitted and required ways of going on within a particular community. The categories of rights and obligations, which are central to social positioning theory, can therefore be employed to refer to the same phenomena as previously described by the category of collective practice. Indeed, Lawson goes so far as to explicitly state:

> [R]ights and obligations [. . .] may [. . .] (and likely do more typically) emerge spontaneously through general human interaction, with rights being implicit in certain widely followed individual actions and with obligations manifest as norms of human activity. Such implicit allowed and required ways of going on, structuring individual actions, can be referred to as collective practices.
>
> (Lawson, 2022, p. 11)

10　For Lawson, the category of human action refers to a behaviour that is governed by reasons. Lawson (1997, p. 173) writes that "human action is governed by reasons so that it is always directed by some beliefs, or knowledge, and towards some end(s)". Moreover, Lawson has explained that he:

> [R]efer[s] to behaviour that is intentional, i.e. behaviour viewed under its aspect of being directed, as action. In other words actions are intentional human doings. The beliefs grounded in the practical interests of life which appear able to motivate actions and make a difference to what occurs (and so must be assessed as functioning causally) I have collected under the heading of reasons. So, in short, in the framework I defend, human actions are simply intentional human doings, meaning doings in the performance of which reasons have functioned causally, where reasons are beliefs grounded in the practical interests of life.
>
> (Lawson, 2003, p. 47)

Such actions are importantly conceptualised by Lawson as having, as a precondition, pre-existing social structure. Lawson (1997, p. 163) writes that "positions and relations are a precondition for intentional action. Because social structure is drawn upon in, and so presupposed by, action it must pre-exist it". Lawson (2003, p. 40) adds that "social structure is both condition of, as well as dependent upon, human action. So it is neither created by, nor creative of, human action". I acknowledge that there is a vast literature providing a variety of conceptualisations of human action. But it is outside the scope of this book to consider such a wealth of conceptions, and their relationship to Lawson's, here. For an interesting overview of different conceptions of action, in particular those informing authors such as Gilbert and Bratman, whom I have cited in Chapter 1 as key contributors to analytic social ontology, see Preston (2013).

11 Such expectations that ways of proceeding will be adhered to are often enforced by more or less formal sanctions. Lawson (2016a, p. 258), for example, writes that where individuals do not follow community-accepted rights and obligations they "would likely be met by one or more of a variety of sanctions including ridicule, contempt, ostracism, aggression, social exclusion, and so on".

12 This is in contrast to a conception such as Searle's that emphasises representations and agreement taking place in individual minds and, as such, Lawson argues, does not acknowledge a practical dimension. Searle's conception implies that social phenomena and deontology come into being only through linguistic declarations and are maintained in existence through collective acceptance that occurs only in the minds of individuals. While Lawson does not deny that such processes are involved, he stresses that they are not exhaustive. For Lawson (2016b, p. 381), "there is more to social existence or institutional reality than linguistic declarations or whatever. There is a material or practical dimension to social reality that grounds the institutional facts that can be generated". Searle, however, fails to recognise this material reality and consequently, according to Lawson (2016b, p. 370), "proposes a more mentalistic or representational approach". Lawson's reading of Searle as missing a practical dimension has informed his work relating to Veblen:

> [I]nstitutions are constituted as habits of thought [. . .] is the correct interpretation of Veblen on these issues. [. . .] I defend an account of social reality that has a greater practical dimension and where social structures include emergent totalities (such as capitalism itself) that are not always well understood, or uncontested, let alone purely ideational (though of course always dependent on human conceptions).
>
> (Lawson, 2014b, p. 999)

He then goes on to say that "if I am now interpreting it correctly, Veblen's notion of institution is seemingly very similar to that currently defended, for example, by John Searle". For more on this, see Martins (2020).

Some, however, have argued that there is indeed a practical dimension to Searle's conception of social ontology. For example, Vicari argues:

[B]oth collective intentionality and language do not "create" *ex novo* human sociality. The human mental architecture, even before the development of language and of the actual occurrence of we-intentional states, is already intersubjectively structured: language and collective intentionality leverage upon this pre-existing sense of sociality and of community to give rise to specific cooperative interactions. The goal of Searle's social ontology, then, if my reading hypothesis is correct, is not to show how a set of mutually, structurally isolated minds can be "put together" in interaction by collective intentionality and language. Rather, collective intentionality and language enact in the public space of reasons an intersubjectivity which is already built into the logical structure of our mental skills.

(Vicari, 2015, p. 195)

Vicari also holds the view that:

The general hypothesis of the Background holds that every intentional state is enabled to determine conditions of satisfaction only if the agent has some relevant preintentional capacities regarding how things are in the world and how to act in the world. Some of these skills are a part of our "deep Background"—that is, they are embodied in our biological structure as human beings (such as the implicit awareness of our motor potentialities)—while others are a part of our "local Background"—that is, they are the result of our embedding in social and cultural relationships in a certain environment (i.e., knowing how to play baseball).

(Vicari, 2015, p. 197)

For Vicari, Searle's notion of the background implies that collective intentionality, and language, always occurs in a pre-existing social context such as a community. Indeed, in Lawson's terms, Vicari's view could be interpreted as Searle considering that individuals are always positioned as components of communities. Therefore, Vicari argues:

[W]hile saying that social behavior and conversation play a key role in the construction of society is [. . .] correct, saying that these phenomena are the "foundation" of society is wrong, since each one of these phenomena presupposes a "form of society" and "some level of sense of community" as one of their necessary conditions.

(Vicari, 2015, p. 199)

Interestingly, one possible interpretation of the differences between Lawson's conception and Searle, which Lawson himself suggests, is that, rather than being an alternative or even opposed to Searle's conception, the conception defended in Cambridge could be considered to complete Searle's theory, which only covers a small part of the process of social constitution:

Though the noted differences are seemingly quite significant I am not convinced that the basic orientations are irreconcilable. Certainly, in emphasising the reality of emergent social totalities and their relational structures I take myself to be supporting a naturalistic account, and at no point would I wish to deny the constituting role of language. Nor do I seek to dispense with the descriptions that Searle calls institutional facts, or with notions of

collective intentionality, etc. But I have argued that it is the former emergent features that ground institutional facts and render them correct or
not, albeit constituting a reality that depends on us and our attitudes and
beliefs though not reducing to them. Searle is clearly reluctant to accept
this assessment. Even so I do not think it challenges Searle's conception so
much as provides, as I say, a practical grounding for it.

(Lawson, 2016b, p. 394)

Lawson never denies that the key elements of Searle's conception are involved
in social constitution. Lawson recognises the importance of collective intentionality—that he conceives of in a manner that is consistent with Searle—
and language, for example. But he argues that this is not the whole story and
that a conception that emphasises such features ends up being mind determined and ignoring the practical dimension, which is equally, if not more,
important.

13 A further interesting component of Lawson's conception is that he draws a
distinction between individual and collective acceptance and characterises individual acceptance as involving two forms, "individual acceptance to partici-
pate" and "individual acceptance of [. . .] merit or legitimacy" (Lawson, 2012,
p. 363). The former involves simply going along with whatever is accepted
whereas the latter involves some form of condoning whatever is accepted. Collective acceptance, then, does not involve the latter.

14 Lawson's conception of collective acceptance is, once again, distinct from Searle's understanding. While Searle (1995) used the terminology of collective acceptance, he later recognises issues with such terminology and suggests that
perhaps using collective recognition would serve his purposes better:

> In earlier writings, I tended to emphasize acceptance, but several commen-
> tators, especially Jennifer Hudin, thought this might imply approval. I did
> not mean it to imply approval. Acceptance, as I construe it, goes all the way
> from enthusiastic endorsement to grudging acknowledgment, even the ac-
> knowledgment that one is simply helpless to do anything about, or reject, the
> institutions in which one finds oneself. So in this book, to avoid this misunder-
> standing, I will use "recognition" or sometimes the disjunction "recognition or
> acceptance". [. . .] I want to emphasize again that "recognition" does not imply
> "approval". Hatred, apathy, and even despair are consistent with the recogni-
> tion of that which one hates, is apathetic toward, and despairs of changing.

(Searle, 2010, p. 8)

Why is the term recognition more appropriate for Searle's purposes? Using the
term recognition works in Searle's case because his conception of collective acceptance or recognition occurs in the mind and implies conscious acknowledgement. The only issue for Searle with using the term acceptance is that the form
of acknowledgement that he is aiming to describe does not imply approval,
which is potentially connoted by the term acceptance. The term recognition,
for Searle, is an appropriate replacement because, in his view, recognising that
something is there does not imply approving of it being there. By removing the
connotation of approval, Searle finds a solution and is able to appropriately
describe a process whereby individual members of a group, through collective
intentionality, think "we recognise Y". The solution, as I showed earlier, is not
as simple for Lawson. For more on the use of the term recognition, see Ikaheimo
and Laitinen (2011).

15 Lawson has even, at times, gone so far as to suggest that trust is the thing that
binds social totalities together, that it is *the* glue, seemingly to the exclusion of
other factors. This has led to criticism. Searle, for example, writes:

Lawson denied that deontic powers were the glue that holds human civilization together. He said that the glue was "trust". In the second paper, he leaves out this claim. Did he change his mind? Trust cannot be a sufficient answer because it does not distinguish between human and animal societies. Animals also have trust, but only humans have deontic powers.

(Searle, 2016, p. 402)

I have no idea whether animals trust and I have already addressed the issues with Searle's criticism of Lawson's framework in terms of applying to both human and animal societies. It is not of Lawson's concern whether or not animals share some human capacities. But Searle has understood Lawson's position to be that trust is *the* glue and that other factors, such as rights and obligations, are not involved. I have previously clarified the relationship between trust and rights and obligations.

16 Lawson interestingly characterises the role of trust using a series of metaphors. He refers to trust as the "glue of social communities". Moreover, Lawson calls trust the adhesive and the binding of the organisational structure:

[T]he role of rights and obligations in structuring social life presupposes the human capacities of being able to be both trustworthy and trusting of others, of being willing and able to make and keep to promises and other commitments, and to believe that others can and will also do so. It should be clear that these human capacities are necessary conditions for the interactions involved to occur, for obligations in particular to be efficacious. As such these capacities of trusting and being trustworthy, etc., qualify as much as anything for being categorised as the glue of social reality, as the adhesive that enables the organisational structure to achieve a degree of binding.

(Lawson, 2015, p. 39)

Lawson has even referred to trust as the cement of communities:

The cement of such groupings [communities] consists especially in the human capacities for trusting and being trustworthy. If, typically, individuals either could not be, or were never, trusted to fulfil their positional obligations, society as we know it would fall apart.

(Lawson, 2014a, p. 4)

17 Pratten, in elaborating this account, draws on the work of Bernstein (2015) and McGeer (2002)

References

Bernstein, J. M. (2015). *Torture and dignity: An essay on moral injury*. Chicago: The University of Chicago Press.

Ikaheimo, H., & Laitinen, A. (Eds.). (2011). *Recognition and social ontology*. Leiden: Brill.

Lawson, T. (1997). *Economics and reality*. London and New York: Routledge.

Lawson, T. (2003). *Reorienting economics*. London and New York: Routledge.

Lawson, T. (2012). Ontology and the study of social reality: Emergence, organisation, community, power, social relations, corporations, artefacts and money. *Cambridge Journal of Economics, 36*(2), 345–385. doi:10.1093/cje/ber050

Lawson, T. (2013). Emergence and morphogenesis: Causal reduction and downward causation? In M. S. Archer (Ed.), *Social morphogenesis* (pp. 61–85). Dordrecht: Springer.

Lawson, T. (2014a). The nature of the firm and peculiarities of the corporation. *Cambridge Journal of Economics, 39*(1), 1–32. doi:10.1093/cje/beu046

Lawson, T. (2014b). Process, order and stability in Veblen. *Cambridge Journal of Economics, 39*(4), 993–1030. doi:10.1093/cje/beu045

Lawson, T. (2014c). A speeding up of the rate of social change? Power, technology, resistance, globalisation and the good society. In M. S. Archer (Ed.), *Late modernity: Trajectories towards morphogenic society*. Dordrecht: Springer.

Lawson, T. (2015). A conception of social ontology. In S. Pratten (Ed.), *Social ontology and modern economics* (pp. 19–52). London and New York: Routledge.

Lawson, T. (2016a). Collective practices and norms. In M. S. Archer (Ed.), *Morphogenesis and the crisis of normativity* (pp. 249–279). Dordrecht: Springer.

Lawson, T. (2016b). Comparing conceptions of social ontology: Emergent social entities and/or institutional facts? *Journal for the Theory of Social Behaviour, 46*(4), 359–399. doi:10.1111/jtsb.12126

Lawson, T. (2016c). Ontology and social relations: Reply to Doug Porpora and to Colin Wight. *Journal for the Theory of Social Behaviour, 46*(4), 438–449. doi:10.1111/jtsb.12128

Lawson, T. (2016d). Social positioning and the nature of money. *Cambridge Journal of Economics, 40*(4), 961–996. doi:10.1093/cje/bew006

Lawson, T. (2016e). Some critical issues in social ontology: Reply to John Searle. *Journal for the Theory of Social Behaviour, 46*(4), 426–437.

Lawson, T. (2019). *The nature of social reality: Issues in social ontology*. London and New York: Routledge.

Lawson, T. (2022). Social positioning theory. *Cambridge Journal of Economics, 46*(1), 1–39. doi:10.1093/cje/beab040

Martins, N. O. (2020). Reconsidering the notions of process, order and stability in Veblen. *Cambridge Journal of Economics, 44*(5), 1115–1135. doi:10.1093/cje/beaa005

McGeer, V. (2002). Developing trust. *Philosophical Explorations, 5*(1), 21–38. doi:10.1080/10002002018538720

Pratten, S. (2017). Trust and the social positioning process. *Cambridge Journal of Economics, 41*(5), 1419–1436. doi:10.1093/cje/bex040

Pratten, S. (2022). Social positioning theory and Dewey's ontology of persons, objects and offices. *Journal of Critical Realism, 21*(3), 288–308. doi:10.1080/14767430.2022.2049091

Preston, B. (2013). *A philosophy of material culture*. London and New York: Routledge.

Searle, J. R. (1969). *Speech acts: An essay in the philosophy of language*. Cambridge: Cambridge University Press.

Searle, J. R. (1979). *Expression and meaning: Studies in the theory of speech acts*. Cambridge: Cambridge University Press.

Searle, J. R. (1983). *Intentionality: An essay in the philosophy of mind*. Cambridge: Cambridge University Press.

Searle, J. R. (1992). *The rediscovery of the mind*. Cambridge, MA: MIT Press.

Searle, J. R. (1995). *The construction of social reality*. London: Penguin.

Searle, J. R. (2001). *Rationality in action*. Cambridge, MA: MIT Press.

Searle, J. R. (2002). *Consciousness and language*. Cambridge: Cambridge University Press.

Searle, J. R. (2010). *Making the social world: The structure of human civilization*. Oxford: Oxford University Press.

Searle, J. R. (2015). Status functions and institutional facts: Reply to Hindriks and Guala. *Journal of Institutional Economics, 11*(3), 507–514. doi:10.1017/s1744137414000629

Searle, J. R. (2016). The limits of emergence: Reply to Tony Lawson. *Journal for the Theory of Social Behaviour, 46*(6), 400–412. doi:10.1111/jtsb.12125

Vicari, G. (2015). Collective intentionality, language, and normativity: A problem and a possible solution for the analysis of cooperation. *Epekeina, 5*(1), 183–207. doi:10.7408/epkn.v5i1.120

5 Social positioning and the formation of community components

The social positioning process involves positions being constituted, or otherwise being made available, within totalities and then items being allocated to, or coming to occupy, those positions. Items are thereby relationally organised with the result being the formation of components of totalities.[1] I have already outlined, in the previous chapter, how positions are constituted in human communities through the elaboration of sets or packages of rights and obligations. Here, I consider the community components that are formed when items are organised by these rights and obligations.

I begin by discussing how items might come to occupy community positions. I then consider the nature of the community components so formed. Key here is the recognition that community components have relational properties that the items that occupy positions do not. It follows that components are irreducible to the items allocated to positions. I then discuss the function and performance of components within communities. I explain that while all community components have functions, the performance of components may vary and, as a result, these functions may exist unserved.

Finally, to illustrate how social positioning theory can provide explanatorily powerful accounts of the natures of different social phenomena, I examine two interesting examples of community component formation involving the positioning of different types of items, namely human persons and whole (sub)communities.[2] First, I consider the process whereby human persons are allocated to gender positions. Second, I examine how a community can be allocated to a person position through the mechanism of legal personhood, drawing on the example of the corporation.[3]

Position occupancy

Positions must be occupied for community components to be formed.[4] In early formulations of social positioning theory, Lawson distinguished three steps to the process through which items are allocated to positions[5] involving notions of practical placement,[6] the harnessing of capacities[7] and the allocation of status.[8] While such features may be involved in specific instances of positional allocation, Lawson (2022, p. 18) has

DOI: 10.4324/9781003110873-5

recognised that these are not requirements for items to occupy positions and, rather, "more or less any item can be allocated to any community position where relevant community participants are prepared to accept or go along with it". In short, how items get allocated to positions will differ from context to context. The only condition that must be satisfied is that community members collectively accept that a position is occupied.

That said, for the sake of illustration, Lawson has provided some broad generalisations as to how positional allocation might occur. For Lawson, the items allocated to positions:

[A]re mostly selected from pre-existing individually distinguishable/ identifiable items where these have been either a) produced and/or fashioned or trained to constitute viable candidates for occupancy of the relevant positions, or b) found to be simply "available" in relevant contexts, with some occupants never having been produced or fashioned for social positioning of any kind at all.

(Lawson, 2022, p. 14)[9]

So, items might be designed, in the case of artefacts, for a particular purpose or an individual may spend a decade or more at universities to obtain a doctorate in the hope of being appointed to a lectureship. But neither design nor training guarantees that an item will be allocated to an intended and/or desired position. Indeed, it is often the case that for human persons positional allocation is subject to numerous barriers to entry:

For most human beings, under current conditions, the task of gaining access to any of many person positions, not least to highly desired or sought-after ones, is practically next to impossible. Certainly, gaining access is typically not a matter simply of choice. Rather it can involve overcoming numerous barriers to entry and/or forms of resistance and (or including) discrimination. The allocation of any person position, in the first instance, is usually in the power of members of some authority positioned in effect as gate keepers that may employ entry criteria of their own. Processes of community position constitution and allocation are mostly highly political in nature.

(Lawson, 2022, p. 19)

That said, items can also simply be in the right place at the right time and be allocated to positions regardless of suitability. Moreover, positional allocation can, and commonly does, occur alongside the constitution of positions such that community components and novel positions emerge simultaneously. Therefore, there can be no general account of how items are allocated or come to occupy community positions and, as such, this feature of the social positioning process would be more appropriately dealt with at the level of empirical research. Indeed, items come to occupy positions in such a variety of ways that it is not possible to provide a set of general necessary principles required for allocation to occur. Rather, the only condition that must be satisfied for an item to be allocated to a position is that community members go along with it.

Community components

Once an item—which may include a kind of artefact, a human person, a whole sub-community or some non-social phenomenon, etc.—occupies a position within a community, a community component is formed. As is the case with the components of any kind of totality, community components have relational properties that the items positioned do not. So, community components, like all components, are both ontologically and causally irreducible to the items out of which they are formed.

Consider the component lecturer of a university community. In that case, the position is the set of rights and obligations that may relate to delivering lectures, marking essays, receiving a salary, having an office and so on. The item that gets positioned is then, in general, a human person—named, say, Sam. When Sam is allocated to the position of lecturer, a component of the totality university is formed that is somewhat distinct from both the position and the item allocated to that position. So, Sam, on being positioned, gives rise to, for example, the component *Lecturer Sam*.[10] *Lecturer Sam* has relational properties given by the package of rights and obligations that make up the lecturer position that Sam does not have. As such, *Lecturer Sam* is not reducible to Sam.[11]

Sam's capacities do come to bear on *Lecturer Sam*. But even if Sam has capacities that would make Sam a good candidate to be allocated to the position of lecturer, until a process of positioning takes place, the component *Lecturer Sam* is not formed. It is only the component formed through positioning—*Lecturer Sam*—that, due to the rights and obligations of the position, is allowed and required to stand up in front of a lecture theatre full of students and teach. So, while the capacities of Sam come to bear on the performance of *Lecturer Sam*, it is the component *Lecturer Sam* who is allowed and required to deliver a lecture.

In addition to such person components, human communities also include non-person or object components. A person component, as illustrated earlier, "possesses or bears, and (where able) may directly exercise or fulfil, the (deontic) powers (rights and obligations) that constitute that position". In contrast, a non-person component "is subjected to the organising influence of matched right/obligation social relations (where they are) only indirectly" by being used by a person component (Lawson, 2022, pp. 11–12).[12] This distinction does not, however, imply that a non-person component is in any way different to person components in terms of its irreducibility nor does it imply that the capacities of the positioned item bear differently on the component formed through positioning. The irreducibility of non-person components is:

> [E]specially apparent where items are allocated to positions clearly very different to those for which they were originally intended, as, say, when a totality built to be a seafaring boat is moored permanently to the banks of the Thames and used (positioned) as a nightclub.
>
> (Lawson, 2022, p. 22)[13]

In such an example, the component *nightclub* is clearly irreducible to the totality built to be a seafaring boat. Indeed, it is also clear that the capacities of the totality qua seafaring boat come to bear on the working of the component *nightclub*—it may, for example, rock from side to side as people dance. So, in all cases, community components are formed where items are organised by social relations in the form of packages or sets of rights and obligations and, as such, community components have relational properties that position occupants do not.

Function and component performance

For Lawson (2022, p. 12), "[e]ach community component is associated with a function, this being an appropriate way of performing that is oriented to facilitating a particular state or characteristic way of working or survival of the wider system or community".[14] Community components are oriented towards realising these functions by the rights and obligations of their associated positions.[15] In other words:

> A function of an entity is roughly what it is supposed to do. With functions being associated with specifically components of totalities, the sorts of actions and uses that are so characterised will be oriented, ultimately, to facilitating particular states or characteristic ways of working, or simply the survival, of the wider systems of which the components are a part.
>
> (Lawson, 2022, pp. 12–13)[16]

These functions are not somehow fixed or predetermined but, rather:

> [T]he specific forms taken by functions, if varying with context, may arise in any of numerous ways including resulting from authoritative declarations or decisions, or simply, and frequently, being determined as those actions or uses (broadly supportive of the characteristic workings of the wider totality) that are currently the most adhered to in the community or relevant subcommunity as revealed in widespread or relevant practice.
>
> (Lawson, 2022, p. 13)

It is then only in relation to such functions that a component:

> [T]hat performs in ways that fail to contribute to sustaining the characteristic way of working of the totality of which it is a part can, *from the perspective of the latter*, be described as performing poorly, or as malfunctioning or even as being dysfunctional, etc.
>
> (Lawson, 2022, p. 4)[17]

Consider, again, the example of the component *Lecturer Sam*. The position lecturer will be constituted by rights and obligations like teaching, marking, research, being paid, having an office and so on. These rights and obligations orientate a component towards the function of, say, conducting and transmitting research which, in turn, supports the overall working of the community, in this case a university.[18] This overall way of working depends on the acceptance of the wider community that a university's role is, for example, producing and transmitting research. Ideally, then, in the case of the component *Lecturer Sam*, the item positioned—Sam—has capacities that bear on the component such that it can serve these functions.

Lawson (2022, p. 20), however, is clear that "it cannot be generally supposed that position occupants do all give rise to component instances that have the capacity to realise associated functions". In the case that Sam lacks appropriate capacities such that *Lecturer Sam* cannot serve the function of conducting and transmitting research, it remains the case that the component *Lecturer Sam* has such a function, it is just that "the associated function exists unrealised" (Lawson, 2022, p. 17).

There is a clear distinction, then, between component formation and the performance of components.[19] If components always have associated functions, components can be formed where the capacities of items positioned do not allow components to perform such that they can fulfil their functions. Indeed, Lawson (2022, p. 19) is clear that "components [. . .] are formed when positions become occupied irrespective of the capacities brought to the positions by their occupants". For even if the aim of the positioning process is to allocate items with appropriate capacities to positions, this does not always occur.

Moreover, it is also the case that even where an item has appropriate capacities, this does not guarantee that the component to which it gives rise will act in a manner that is consistent with the rights and obligations of the position and so serve the component's function. Indeed, the "actions of any particular person component instance may depart, possibly significantly, from those in line with its (component) powers (the associated positional rights and obligations)" (Lawson, 2022, p. 17). But neither this lack of capacity or conduct that diverges from that of the rights and obligations of the position do, in and of themselves, mean that components are not formed.

It is possible that not performing a function may result in an item being removed from a position, but this will not always be the case:

> [W]here, for whatever reason, a component instance does not perform in a particular expected manner or to the desired standard, the position occupant may be replaced. But whether, and if so how quickly, this happens is a matter that will vary from case to case. So long as the person or item in question continues to occupy the relevant position [. . .] the corresponding component instance remains in place.
>
> (Lawson, 2022, p. 19)

Moreover, exiting a position, or removing an occupant, is not always straightforward:

> [D]e-positioning does not follow simply from poor performance, and nor, in the case of person positions, is it usually simply the choice of the individuals involved. Rather, the exiting of person positions very often requires effective community acceptance, as, in many communities, in getting a marriage divorce, having an offered resignation accepted, being transferred to another football team, leaving a gang or the military, [. . .] etc.
>
> (Lawson, 2022, p. 19)

What difference, then, does the performance of components make? The answer is that "[w]hether it matters that an instance of a community component is considered to serve an associated component function (well) will vary with context and from case to case" (Lawson, 2022, p. 18). So, for example, a football player may remain injured and unable to serve their associated component functions of playing football for their club for many years while still remaining employed at the club with all of the associated rights and obligations. In contrast, if a lawnmower breaks and is unable to mow the lawn, it is likely that the person component that owns the lawnmower will replace it quickly. Questions, therefore, relating to the effects of the performance of different specific components require empirical research. In terms of the nature of community components, these are formed where an item comes to occupy a position and these components always have functions regardless of capacities or performance.

In short, community components are formed where an item occupies a position. Each component is irreducible to the item out of which it is formed. But the capacities of the item bear on the performance of the component. There are non-person and person components. The rights and obligations associated with non-person components bear on their uses but are exercised person components. Person components may directly access their rights and obligations. Each component is associated with a function, but its constitution as a component does not depend on its performance of this function.

Examples of community component formation

There is only so much that can be said about social positioning theory at the level of general principles. Indeed, as explained earlier, many aspects of the theory are best elaborated through empirical research or by examining the natures of specific social existents. Therefore, I turn now to consider briefly, from the perspective of social positioning theory, two examples of social phenomena that have been of particular interest to social scientists, social theorists and philosophers: gender and the corporation.

Gender

When a human person is allocated to a person position, a corresponding person component is formed within a community. Person components may directly access or exercise the rights and obligations of their position. These rights and obligations orientate the person component towards serving a function that supports the overall working of the totality and are matched to the rights and obligations of other components within the totality. Perhaps the most straightforward examples of this process are, as drawn upon above, formal positions such as various jobs:

> [I]ndividuals positioned, say, as employees in a modern UK firm may each acquire an obligation to be in some workplace at certain times, and usually be required to engage in various practices. At the same time, the employees will acquire rights to remuneration for the hours spent in the workplace, as well as perhaps various others regarding health and safety measures and insurance. Or where individuals become positioned as university students, they obtain rights to attend lectures and obligations to produce results of study and sit exams, and so forth. All such positional rights and obligations ensure that system functions are served.
>
> (Lawson, 2019b, p. 14)

It would be wrong, however, to think of this process as operating only in contexts in which we are allocated to jobs or otherwise formally appointed to various positions. Rather, as explained in Chapter 3, "[w]e are all born into some or other set of communities" and "we interact as human beings only as participants in a number of communities" (Lawson, 2022, p. 7). We exist only as formed into person components and we are, therefore, shaped from the moment that we are born by positions that, in many cases, we have not chosen nor even are aware of when first allocated to them.[20] One such position to which we are mostly, if not all, allocated to at birth that greatly impacts our lives is gender. How then does social positioning theory account for gender?[21]

For Lawson, there is a set of gender positions, which have increased in number over time, to which human persons are allocated. The gender positions to which human persons are most commonly allocated are gendered woman and gendered man. Let us consider the position of gendered man. In terms of its constitution, the position gendered man is characterised in many communities by a disproportionately large number of allowed ways of proceeding that are not made available to all other genders. Many of these are informal but may include, for example, the fact that until relatively recently in many communities the right to vote in elections was a right that belonged only to adults in the position gendered man. Central here is that the rights and obligations constituting the position gendered man are, in most communities, such that the position occupant is privileged throughout the community to the detriment of the remaining gender positions. In other words:

> Gender, of course, is itself a structure of positions and gendering is always a community-based positioning process. And in very many communities, rights and obligations associated with, and indeed in part serving to constitute, the gender position of woman, have long served to disadvantage those so positioned. Those allocated, on whatever biological or any other basis, to the position *gendered woman* are simply allocated rights and obligations that mostly (certainly frequently) serve to disadvantage the position occupants relative to others gender-positioned differently, in ways that have nothing to do with intrinsic or biological capabilities of those so positioned. The very process of gender positioning has itself been discriminatory.
>
> (Lawson, 2019b, pp. 235–236)

How, then, does a person come to occupy the position gendered man? While the process varies, it is perhaps most commonly the case that human infants—at the moment of birth and even sometimes before—are allocated to the position "in ways that have nothing to do with matching capacities to position requirements and opportunities" but, rather, by parents and other person components of the relevant community typically perhaps "according to [. . .] perceived reproductive capacities" on the basis that the child has certain physical characteristics, in this case perhaps through possessing a penis (Lawson, 2022, p. 23). Once positioned, the person component may directly access the privileges of a gendered man even if initially, with children lacking the capacities to exercise these rights and obligations, access will come in the form of differential—often preferential—treatment on the part of parents and other person components of the relevant community. It is therefore often the case that by the time a person positioned as a gendered man is able to themselves directly exercise the rights and ob-ligations of their position, they are so accustomed to the privileges of the position that they are unable to recognise either that such advantages are relational properties and not intrinsic to themselves or that human persons occupying different gender positions do not all benefit from the same rights and obligations.

Gender is an example in which the conflation between community com-ponent and item positioned is particularly common, on the part of both the positioned person and members of wider community. This is a mistake that must be avoided because reducing the gendered component to the human person that is positioned can cause and has caused significant harm:

> One such case of substantial political/ethical harm that, in the case of the positioning of specifically human beings, results from this errone-ous ontological reduction is everywhere in evidence. This is a masking of the basis of long-lasting gender [. . .] discriminations that prevail in most communities and are certainly prevalent in the modern UK. For it is not unusual to find many community participants, even those faced with the most limited range of opportunities, as well as commentators on the topic, attributing (erroneously) the varying qualities of life expe-riences, lifestyles and levels or standards of well-being, that reflect the unequal distributions of opportunities and powers that characterise cer-tain *positions* of gender [. . .] to supposed differential intrinsic capacities of position *occupants*. With individuals in practice mostly allocated to a specific gender [. . .] positions according to factors such as (prevailing interpretations of) biological or physical markings or families or loca-tions of origin, the consequence is, in effect, a perpetuation of erroneous (naïve) forms of biological essentialism.
>
> (Lawson, 2022, p. 23)

While it is beyond the scope of this book to detail the nature of such a system of discrimination,[22] let alone to consider strategies for emancipa-tory practice,[23] it is important to highlight that central to being able to identify the existence of such issues is a recognition of difference between community components and the items out of which they are formed. It is due to the relational properties given by the position gendered man that gendered men qua community components have advantages that are not afforded to those who are gendered differently. The privileges enjoyed by gendered men are not linked to any particular capacities of the persons so positioned. As human persons only ever exist as components of commu-nities, these relational features of the component and the capacities of the person positioned are often conflated. Social positioning theory serves to make clear the difference between the item positioned and the resulting community component and, as such, one can avoid mistaken ontological reductions.

Corporations

It is possible for whole (sub)communities to be positioned as components of wider communities,[24] giving rise to either a non-person or a person component.[25] When a community is allocated to a non-person position, the rights and obligations of the position are as with all non-person positions, not accessed by the resulting non-person component but, rather, these rights and obligations may be exercised by person components of both the wider community and the positioned (sub)community.[26] My focus, here, however, is when a community is allocated to a person position, which, as I show, can and does happen. When this occurs, the result is the formation a person component of the wider community, one that may directly access the rights and obligations that constitute the position.

The most common example of a community coming to occupy a person position, at least in contemporary societies,[27] is the corporation.[28] To understand this process, the first notion to grasp is that of legal fiction. According to Lawson, a legal fiction is:

> [B]asically a false claim about a pertaining situation to which the legal process resorts for purposes of adjusting the incidence of a pre-existing (set of) rule(s). If we think of all legal rules in a specific community as applying to a given set of situations, then it is possible in law to extend the application of legal rules to an additional set of situations in that same community by misrepresenting these additional situations as conforming to those of the set for which the legal rule was originally intended, *even though in reality they do not*. The misrepresentation of the facts of these situations in order that a pre-existing rule can be applied to them is known as a legal fiction.
>
> (Lawson, 2014, p. 18)[29]

In the case of the formation of corporations, the relevant legal fiction is that of a legal person, which is the "position to which non-human entities are allocated in order to obtain the right to acquire other rights and obligations" (Lawson, 2014, p. 29). Nested, then, within the position legal person is the more specific position of corporation. If a community is allocated to that position, it becomes incorporated, giving rise to a corporation, which as a legal person possesses a particular set of rights and obligations that is a subset of those originally intended only for human person components. As such, rights and obligations that would otherwise be directly accessed by the individuals involved in the company are transferred to the corporation itself.[30] Examples of such rights and obligations include "owning assets (houses, boats, shares etc.), contracting, suing and being sued, and so on" (Lawson, 2019b, p. 135). Therefore, the community qua corporation—not the individuals that constitute the community—may, for example, own property or other corporations. The result is a separation between the rights and obligations that are those of the positioned community and the rights and obligations that are those of the individuals that constitute the positioned community.

Attributing the right to own property to the positioned community qua corporation then allows for the creation of the kind of multinational structures that are characteristic of many contemporary corporations:

> [A]ny corporation can establish a set of separate entities, perhaps situated in different countries, legally own the latter's shares and thereby constitute each of the latter as (seemingly partly or wholly owned) subsidiaries, each with a separate legal status, where any such subsidiary can also spawn further subsidiaries *ad infinitum*. This means that a mechanism is in place for generating structures that provide opportunities for endlessly transferring liabilities in a dazzling variety of ways.
>
> (Lawson, 2019b, pp. 140–141)

Moreover, the separation of rights and obligations means that the individuals running, or otherwise involved with, the corporation very rarely find themselves being held responsible for decisions or actions taken in relation to that corporation:

> [W]here a company *is* found liable for something, it cannot be imprisoned or set to work in the community; in practice the only punishment typically metered out is a fine, something it can usually easily afford, the expectation of which will frequently have been built into its undertakings. If, however, there are circumstances where a company cannot pay its fines, or it otherwise seeks to avoid doing so, the losers will not be the shareholders. For limited liability means, as we have seen, that the shareholders are not responsible for the company's debts beyond the value of shares yet to be paid. Nor can shareholders be held responsible for any civil or criminal offences that may have been committed. Rather, in such cases the company typically avoids paying not only its numerous creditors, but also any wages that may be owed to workers as well as civil damages. Meanwhile, and for essentially the same reasons, corporate decision makers are extremely unlikely to be held responsible for the consequences of the corporate mechanism. So a company, or its set of director agents, ultimately has every incentive for it, or one of its subsidiaries, to take manifestly irresponsible, potentially damaging, and even life threatening, risks where the possible potential benefits are significant. Indeed, if or where it is maintained (however erroneously) that there exists a legal obligation for the corporation to serve the financial interests of its shareholders [. . .] it could well be argued that they ought to. For where the risks pay off in the

> sense that significant profits are realised, the shareholders benefit
> substantially; where things go wrong, even terribly so, these same
> shareholders have very limited liability.
>
> (Lawson, 2015c, p. 225)

Clearly any actions that are taken, which are attributed to the corporation, are in fact performed by individuals qua person components of the positioned community. But the responsibilities and consequences associated with such actions are removed from those individuals and attributed to the positioned community, with, quite unsurprisingly, potentially damaging results. Once again, it is beyond the scope of this book to go into detail as to the endlessly complex arrangements made possible by attributing legal personhood to a community qua corporation. But it is only possible to understand such structures by first recognising the distinction that exists between the community that is positioned and the package of rights and obligations by which it is organised. Social positioning theory serves to identify that as long as there is collective acceptance on the part of relevant community members, it is possible to grant direct access to rights and obligations, which is generally reserved for human persons, to an entity that is manifestly not a human person.

Concluding remarks

Social positioning theory, at its most basic, is the assessment that at the heart of all social constitution are processes whereby different items come to be relationally organised, giving rise to components of social totalities. Indeed, the theory considers that such organisational processes are at the heart of all constitution, whether social or non-social. In terms of specifically social phenomena, the theory aims to account for the constitution of all social totalities, that is all kinds of organised systems that depend necessarily on us to come into being. Social totalities include artefacts, language systems, human communities, etc. Of these different types of social totalities, the focus of the theory so far has been to provide an account of the constitution of human communities.

In general terms, the social positioning process involves a position being constituted, or becoming available, and the allocation of an item to the position resulting in the formation of a component. In communities, positions are constituted as packages of rights and obligations. These rights and obligations come into being either through declaration or through practice. Items can be allocated to those positions in a variety of ways and are so positioned where community members collectively accept, or go along with, that position occupancy. Once a position is occupied, a community component is formed. These components are irreducible to the items out of which they are formed even if the capacities of those items bear on the components' performance. Each component is then oriented by the rights and obligations of its position towards a function that serves the overall working of the totality—the community—that they in part constitute.

The processes described by social positioning theory can be widely observed and in nature are fairly straightforward. Indeed, it is because they are straightforward that they can be iterated over and over again. So, the scope of the theory is significant. Many of the problems that beset social theory stem, I believe, at least in part, from conflating positioned items with the components to which they give rise and, as such, mistakenly interpreting certain properties or capacities as essential to particular items when, in fact, these properties exist in virtue of relational properties. But social positioning theory draws attention to these sorts of errors by making clear that distinctions must always be maintained between items positioned, the rights and obligations of the positions and the resulting community components that are formed.

The ongoing evolution of the theory within the Cambridge Social Ontology Group will undoubtedly continue through the process that has brought it to this point. Developments in philosophical social ontology inform advances in scientific social ontology, the results of which then come to bear on social positioning theory in a dialectical process of continual development. Projects such as those exploring the natures of technology, money, corporations and gender will continue deploying the latest developments in social positioning theory, with their results in turn being brought to bear on the principles of the theory as, at every CSOG meeting, they are continually questioned. My primary aim with this book is to make the basic framework and its insights more accessible to all. The hope is that this will enable many more to engage with the theory and contribute to its critical scrutiny and development.

Notes

1 Lawson has also expressed these principles as follows:

> The positioning process turns on the application of just two elements or *principles*. These can be iterated over and again in processes of social reality constitution, giving rise to formations that are increasingly intricate. Simply formulated, they are as follows: (1) Within an existing or emerging totality, a novel place, site, slot, space, or opening etc. is created, or an existing one is made (or becomes) available, that is structured in a manner to orient any person or thing allocated to it to serving some system function. (2) Some person or other entity (sometimes a community) is allocated to the place or slot etc., thereby becoming incorporated as a component of the totality or system in a manner oriented to serving a function of the wider totality. The place or site etc. is a social *position*, and the person or entity allocated to it is the position *occupant*. *Social positioning* is a term for *both* steps or principles combined, each presupposing, and oriented to, the other. Very often the position is given a name—P, say—and each occupant thereupon usually acquires a status of, or relating to, P, to indicate occupancy of the relevant position.
>
> (Lawson, 2019b, p. 12)

2 That is not to say that these are the only phenomena that are positioned as components of communities. Non-social phenomena are, for example, often incorporated as components of communities. Research has also been conducted to
determine if other types of phenomena could be positioned. Lawson, for example, has discussed whether practices could be positioned:

> [A] *practice* [. . .] is [. . .] a way of proceeding or going on that is actually
> pursued or followed. Here the emphasis is on both a *way* of proceeding
> as well as on the fact of it actually being followed. If I am engaged in
> the activity of eating an apple or running for a train, such activities may
> not yet be practices. If I regularly peel an apple before eating it, this may
> constitute a practice, a way of eating the apple, or at least for preparing
> it for eating.
>
> (Lawson, 2016a, p. 252)

Lawson then suggests that such individual practices can become collective practices if they are accepted—in the sense I discussed in the previous chapter—by
all members of a community. So, Lawson (2016a, p. 253) argues that a collective
practice is a "practice that in effect has the status of being accepted as legitimate
for the circumstances within the community" and seemingly equates the process
of collective acceptance to that of positioning, writing:

> [A] collective practice is a practice that in effect carries the status of be-
> ing accepted in a particular sense within a particular community. In this
> it is accepted as being proper or legitimate in some way. But this is just
> another way of saying that various individual practices have been so-
> cially positioned; they have in this case been positioned as (versions of) a
> specific collective practice.
>
> (Lawson, 2016a, p. 253)

Lawson no longer considers it possible to position practices.
3 A further example that I do not consider in this chapter but that has been considered at length by Lawson is money. For more on his positioning theory
of money, see Ingham (2018); Lawson (2016c, 2018a, 2018b, 2019a, 2022) and
Searle (2017).
4 Lawson has at times acknowledged the possible existence of unoccupied
positions:

> [T]here are cases where it might be said that a (very real) position (status)
> exists unoccupied. But these are usually temporary at best; for the posi-
> tions are created precisely in order that they be occupied so that certain
> intrinsic capacities of the occupier might be harnessed in order to serve
> some system function. An example is where a position has but a single
> occupant at any given point in time, and the most recent incumbent dies
> or resigns or otherwise exits it, or a positioned artefact malfunctions and
> is removed, etc. But then, typically, the departing occupant is replaced
> as soon as is convenient, given the rules of positioning, or availability of
> alternatives, etc. Otherwise, as I say, excepting in cases of over determina-
> tion, the relevant system functions cannot be served.
>
> (Lawson, 2016b, pp. 382–383)

5 Lawson, for example, explains that:

> [O]bjects, persons or other phenomena: 1) become practically placed or
> arranged or otherwise incorporated (as components of the relevant so-
> cial totalities or systems); 2) have certain sets of capacities, *already pos-
> sessed*, harnessed to serve as one or more system functions; and 3) acquire

(usually) specific statuses within the relevant communities (very often, as I say, identical to the name given to the position itself).

(Lawson, 2019b, p. 13)

The first published instance of the process of positional allocation being set out this way can be traced to Lawson's analysis of the nature of money:

Social positioning is the term for the process whereby, through general acceptance throughout a community, human individuals, things or other phenomena become incorporated as components of these emergent totalities. In all cases, social positioning involves the generalised acceptance of the following three elements regarding any item that is thereby positioned: (i) the allocation of an agreed status; (ii) its practical placement as a component of a totality; and (iii) the harnessing of certain of its capacities *already possessed* to serve as one or more system functions of the totality.

(Lawson, 2016c, p. 963)

6 Previously, Lawson characterised the allocation of items to positions as involving the practical placement of items as components of totalities. Central to this assessment is not a notion of practical placement but rather the idea that items are positioned and as such form components of totalities. The role that *practical placement* plays in the description is merely to make clear that positioning is not a metaphor. Indeed, Lawson (2016d, p. 427) is clear that "any object, person or phenomenon positioned in any way i) is practically placed as a component of a totality (so that in my account the term position is not a metaphor)". In what sense, then, is it not a metaphor? One interpretation has been that the emphasis on *practical placement* carries connotations of movement and incorporation in a physical sense. This may be due to the fact that Lawson often uses examples of the positioning of items resulting in the constitution of components of artefacts to illustrate the positioning process, such as a pane of glass being positioned within a gap in a wall as a window.

For example, Lawson writes:

When an object is simply physically incorporated as a component (*not* of a community directly, but) of an artefact—as with inserting a pane of glass in a space for a window in a wall of house, or a wooden block in a space for a door of the same house—the "opening" created is typically so oriented physically that the mere placement of an appropriate object within it ensures that relevant capacities possessed can be drawn on.

(Lawson, 2019b, p. 13)

Another commonly used example by Lawson (2012, p. 376) to illustrate the positioning process where the movement and physical placement of an object is central is "large sea pebbles, say, being positioned as paperweights". In the case of the paperweight, the pebble is positioned as a paperweight when it is placed on top of a pile of paper and weighs it down. In such examples, Lawson does argue that positioning involves physical movement and placement. For the pane of glass, it becomes a window when it is placed within the hole in the wall. But it would be a mistake to think this is Lawson's meaning in general when using the term practical placement. While an item may be displaced in order to be positioned, particularly in the case of the constitution of artefacts, displacement is not a general requirement for an item to be allocated to a position or often even meaningful. Indeed, in the case of community constitution, the positions involved are never only spatial locations but, rather, as identified in the previous chapter, sets of rights and obligations.

So, what does practical placement imply when one is allocated to a set of rights and obligations? Here, Lawson is using *practical placement* to draw a clear distinction between a conception such as Searle's that is mind-determined and his own. When one is allocated to a set of rights and obligations, one is organised as a component of a community in which one is allowed and required to partake in a whole series of actions that will be matched by the actions of other members of the community. This is a conception that, while minds are involved and therefore is mind-dependent, it is not mind-determined and always recognises, as underlined in the previous chapter, a practical dimension to social constitution. *Practical placement* served to underline this difference. If Lawson no longer employs the terminology of *practical placement*, it is because it is at best redundant and at worst it can lead to misunderstanding. Once it is understood that all positioning involves the incorporation of elements to form components of social totalities and this is not just something that exists in the mind, the emphasis on *practical placement* becomes unnecessary. Furthermore, there is the risk that *practical placement* is interpreted as involving some kind of spatial element, which is not always the case. It has, therefore, been judged unnecessary to retain that terminology.

7 Previously, Lawson emphasised that the capacities of the items that are positioned had to be harnessed such that they served a function within a social totality for those items to be positioned. Moreover, Lawson has at times emphasised that the capacities harnessed were always pre-existing, which has at times caused some confusion. For example, Searle has stated:

> The difficulty I have with this account is the notion that the capacities must already be possessed. There are many forms of status functions where the entity that has the status function does not have the capacity to perform the function prior to the assignment of the status. [...] [E]ntities that are capable of performing functions once a status has been assigned to them, but not capable prior to the assignment, are "limited liability corporations" and so called "fiat" money, what I have been calling "baseless" money.
>
> (Searle, 2017, p. 1467)

Lawson often emphasised the notion of pre-existing capacities when illustrating the positioning of items to form components of artefacts:

> [P]anes of glass may be positioned (identified and practically placed) as windows in a house and blocks of wood as doors, etc. In this process, certain capacities of the positioned objects get to serve as system (here house) functions. Thus, amongst the numerous capacities of each pane of glass is that of allowing light to pass through whilst resisting most of the elements that constitute weather. On being positioned as a window, it is the noted capacity that comes to serve as the glass pane's system/ house function. Similarly, a block of wood may be identified as a door and placed specifically at the "entrance" to a house and get to function as a door does because of capacities already possessed by the item so positioned.
>
> (Lawson, 2016c, p. 964)

Such examples make it quite clear that the capacities that are harnessed are those of the objects that are positioned. A pane of glass does not acquire the capacity of allowing light to pass through by being positioned. A block of wood does not become solid by being placed in a doorway. The capacities that allow these elements to perform the function once positioned pre-exist the positioning. Indeed, these elements are so positioned precisely to harness these pre-existing capacities. With these examples, the idea that pre-existing capacities are harnessed seems relatively uncontentious.

It has been recognised, however, over time, that purely in terms of social constitution it is not necessary for an item to have capacities such that it can serve the function of the position to which it is allocated. Indeed, even in somewhat earlier work Lawson had begun to recognise that capacities were not always harnessed in processes of social positioning:

> [I]f something *lacking* the relevant capacities to successfully function as some X is nevertheless so positioned anyway, then the positioned occupant will very often still be regarded as an X (if retaining position occupancy), albeit as a non- or dysfunctional one; mistakes, or inappropriate acts of positioning, etc., happen. However, where design or decision is actively involved, the goal typically is to position in a way that facilitates the successful functioning of a wider system or totality (through the successful functioning of each component).
>
> (Lawson, 2018a, p. 853)

8 Previously, Lawson argued that the allocation process involved positioned items acquiring an identity or status:

> [A]n individual becomes (acquires the identity of) a university professor, prime minister, or taxi driver, etc., on being collectively accepted/recognised as having gained (legitimate) occupancy of the position Professor, Prime Minister, Taxi Driver, etc. [. . .]. Similarly an artefact becomes (acquires the identity of) a table, cash, passport, and so on, on being collectively accepted/recognised as positioned as such.
>
> (Lawson, 2016b, p. 361)

In such passages it could be interpreted that Lawson is claiming that a table is only a table due to being incorporated as such as a component of a community. Indeed, Lawson has gone so far as to argue that:

> When [. . .] artefacts are particularly complicated and designed to perform a single complicated task, it may appear that they take on the relevant identities independently of being positioned in a human system/community. But ultimately this is not so. If, for example, an object manufactured to be positioned as a photocopier is washed up on an isolated island and some exotic tribe that inhabits the island (and which perhaps lacks a concept of electricity) positions the object in question as a table, then in this particular community a table is what it is. (Similarly a human individual may spend the entirety of her or his formative years training to be a professor, prime minister, opera singer, professional cricketer, Olympic skier or whatever, but unless, or until, they are appropriately positioned they do not take on the status of a member of that position or kind.)
>
> (Lawson, 2014, p. 9)

Lawson, however, has been persuaded over time that it is possible for artefacts to have identities that are constituted independently of positioning. This has largely been as a result of a critique of Lawson's previous position elaborated by Clive Lawson, who argues:

> [T]hat position and identity do not always go together either, or at least not unless a very broad conception of positioning is adopted. For example, whilst it makes sense to talk of positioning a pane of glass within a building's wall as so giving it the function of a window, positioning a complex engine within a racing car does not seem to work in the same way. Is it not also an engine whilst in the manufacturer's box? Thus can it be positioned outside the system in which it is supposed to function?

And so, at what point does it become positioned? Is this once it receives a box with a label, or a safety check, a warrantee? Crucially, can the artefact obtain its identity whilst still under construction or even at the design stage, and so prior to any use whatsoever?

(C. Lawson, 2017, pp. 75–76)

For Clive Lawson, this is particularly apparent in the case of artefacts that are constituted so as to serve a very specific purpose such as:

[A] photocopier. The most striking feature of a photocopier is its physical or constitutional complexity but functional simplicity. Many different parts all come together to do one fairly obvious thing; paper and ink is put in at one end and returned, as a copy, at the other. There may come a time when archaeologists are uncovering the remains of our current civilisation and working out what all our artefacts are for. A passport may be subject to a range of interpretations [. . .], the photocopier (if one survives intact) will more likely not. It should be pretty clear what a photocopier is for. This is because its intrinsic capacities, or physical make-up, tell us so much of the story. Of course, to be "functional" it must always be positioned. It must be used by individuals who know how to use it, be plugged into an electrical system, etc. And it can always be used for other things—it could be sat on, used to hide a hole in the wall, etc. But it is still possible to work out what that artefact was designed for by investigating the structure of the artefact itself, with little recourse to the system within which it is used.

(C. Lawson, 2017, pp. 89–90)

Lawson now makes clear that he recognises that if the positioning process results in the allocation of a positional identity, there are other forms of identity that are also relevant to social constitution. To illustrate, in case of human persons, the component formed through positioning acquires a positional identity:

In these cases [lecturers and students in a university community [. . .] employers and employees in some place of work, the medical staff and patients in a hospital], all those involved acquire a (positional) status or identity—lecturer, student, doctor, nurse, patient, etc.

(Lawson, 2022, p. 21)

In the case of artefacts, it may well be that a similar process occurs in some instances, but Lawson (2022, p. 14) now recognises that artefacts, previous to their allocation to specific community positions, "are often pre-sorted into categories, frequently acquiring (artefactual) identities (of lawn mowers, photocopiers, cars) independently of their occupying positions". The role of identity in the positioning process is, therefore, no longer emphasised to the same extent in elaborating the key features of the process. While elements acquire positional identities through the positioning process, how this occurs and its importance in terms of the constitution of different components will vary from context to context. And in terms of allocation, items such as artefacts may well already have identities before they are positioned. For other views of CSOG members on these issues, see Faulkner, Lawson, and Runde (2010) and Faulkner and Runde (2009, 2013).

9 Lawson, here, is differentiating between fashioned and given occupants. For Lawson (2022, p. 14), fashioned occupants can "be very general in nature (panes of glass, wooden boards etc.) and so fashioned to be candidates for any of a range of positions; others (photocopiers, cars) will form very specific types of candidates", whereas given occupants "include items constructed as artefacts

intended for some other uses, that are repurposed" or, more generally, items that have "come into being for reasons quite unconnected to their eventual positioning".

10 Items that are positioned can, of course, and often do, occupy multiple positions. Where this occurs, "[e]ach such case of positioning results in the formation of a different component" (Lawson, 2022, p. 16). So, if Sam is positioned to give rise to a lecturer and is also positioned to give rise to a fast bowler on a cricket team, two different components are formed, *Lecturer Sam* and *Fast Bowler Sam*. These two components are both are irreducible to Sam. In this example, these are different positions and so components are formed in different communities, say a university and a cricket team.

It is also the case that multiple positioning can occur where positions are nested. A nested position, for Lawson, is one that is constituted in terms of the rights and obligations of another position—the nesting position—along with a number of additional rights and obligations. For example, in the United Kingdom, the Member of Parliament position nests the Prime Minister position, which includes the rights and obligations of the Member of Parliament position, along with a substantial number of additional rights and obligations. When a position is nested "the party entering it is formed into a component of the wider position, where it is the latter component, qua component, that is positioned in the nested position, forming a more specific component of a relevant community" (Lawson, 2022, p. 16). So, say Sam is allocated to the position of Member of Parliament, giving rise to the component *Sam MP*, it is then the component, *Sam MP*, that is allocated to the position of Prime Minister, giving rise to the component *PM Sam*.

Position nesting within communities, however, is not limited to person positions. Non-person positions can also be nested within wider nesting non-person positions:

> Community nonperson or object positions can nest other nonperson positions in the sense that that alongside any set of rights and obligations (associated with person positions) that bear on the (allowed and required) uses of all positioned occupants of some nonperson position X, there can be an additional set of rights and obligations that bear on additional (allowed and required) uses that apply to only a subset of positioned occupants of X. This additional set of rights and obligations thus characterises a further nonperson position, Y say, that is nested within the wider position X, and associated with its own specific function.
>
> (Lawson, 2022, p. 16)

The example that Lawson (2022, p. 22) draws on most regularly to illustrate non-person position nesting is "where (an object positioned as) a Cambridge College dining room table, seemingly identical to all others in the dining room, is used (is further positioned) as a high table". In this example, in a Cambridge college dining room, there are a number of tables positioned to form college dining tables, which will all be used for eating upon. During formal dinners, however, one of these college dining tables will be positioned as the high table that only certain individuals will be allowed to sit at. The nesting position—college dining table—nests the position—high table—which includes the uses of the nesting position plus a series of extra restrictions.

11 Sam is, of course, also irreducible to *Lecturer Sam*. The human person is not exhausted by the positions that they occupy.

12 Lawson previously framed this contrast not in terms of the difference between person and non-person components but in terms of the difference between

when a person is allocated to a position and when a non-person is allocated to a position, such as an artefact:

> [W]hen an *artefact* is positioned as, for example, a traffic beacon, car park or identity card, certain of its capacities become interpreted as its (positional) functions within and relative to the system in which they are positioned, and their use in this is governed by rights and obligations that fall on wider community participants. However, when a *human individual* is positioned as, for example, a judge or prison officer, it is the positioned individual herself or himself that becomes the bearer or agent of novel positional powers and specifically rights and obligations. So the positioning of human beings is also functional. However, in this case of human positioning it is primarily the case that the organising rights and obligations are accessed by those that are positioned.
>
> (Lawson, 2019b, p. 92)

If this is similar, it is not the same as Lawson's current explanation outlined earlier. Indeed, Lawson could be read here as indicating that it is the "human individual"—the item that gets positioned—that acquires or comes to bear the rights and obligations of the position. That is not the case. As I explained earlier, it is the component that either exercises, in the case of person components, or is subjected to, in the case of non-person components, the rights and obligations of the position.

13   Pratten also provides the example of:

> [A] table, effectively identical to others used in the venue, being designated at a wedding reception as the Head table, the table is thereby formed into a community component where its use is constrained by rights and obligations borne by the variously positioned individuals. The participants at the reception interact with the table quite differently. The uses of the Head table do not follow from its intrinsic physical make up but are rather socially sanctioned by the differential rights and obligations falling on the various kinds of participants at the reception. The social positioning of such items means that, when considered as community components, they are never reducible to that which became relationally organised in forming them as components.
>
> (Pratten, 2023, p. 3)

14   Searle argues that notions of a "characteristic way of working" are observer relative and therefore a function is merely an interpretation that we, or some other type of observer, make as to the purpose of some set of causes. In other words, for Searle, the notion of function is all in the mind. Causes only serve the functioning of a system insofar as we determine, in our minds, what a system is for and, consequently, how the causal capacities of a constitutive element act towards that invented end. Searle illustrates this argument by considering the example of the heart pumping blood:

> [G]iven that we already accept that for organisms there is a value in survival and reproduction, and that for a species there is a value in continued existence, we can discover that the function of the heart is to pump blood, the function of vestibular ocular reflex is to stabilise the retinal image, and so on. When we discover such a natural function, there are no natural facts discovered beyond the causal facts. [. . .] It is because we take it for granted in biology that life and survival are values that we can discover the function of the heart is to pump blood. If we thought the most important value in the world was to glorify God by making thumping noises, then the function of the heart would be to make a thumping

noise, and the noisier heart would be the better heart. If we valued death and extinction above all, then we would say that a function of cancer is to speed death. The function of aging would be to hasten death, and the function of natural selection would be extinction. In all these functional assignments, no new intrinsic facts are involved. As far as nature is concerned intrinsically, there are no functional facts beyond causal facts. The further assignment of function is observer relative.

(Searle, 1995, pp. 15–16)

Indeed, for Searle, the term function is distinct from that of cause only insofar as it refers to this additional, value-oriented, perspective given by human beings. The only other possible interpretation, Searle argues, would be for function to be synonymous with cause, and therefore there would be no need for an additional term:

Either "function" is defined in terms of causes, in which case there is nothing intrinsically functional about functions, they are just causes like any others. Or functions are defined in terms of the furtherance of a set of values that we hold—life, survival, reproduction, health—in which case they are observer relative.

(Searle, 1995, pp. 15–16)

15 Lawson (2012, p. 361), to be clear, does "not wish to imply a functionalist explanatory orientation". Lawson explains:

[W]here a positioned individual or object happens at some stage to serve a particular (system) function, this fact in itself should not be thought automatically to explain the emergence of the position or of its occupant(s). How and why things emerge and the paths whereby they end up functioning as they do, rather, are always matters for historical study, i.e. it is a mistake to adopt rationalistic/functionalist styles of analysis.

(Lawson, 2016c, p. 964)

16 In earlier work, Lawson illustrated the functions of different entities by focusing on the contribution that the causal capacities of different positioned items made to the totality in which they were organised. For example, Lawson considered how differently positioned objects might facilitate having a meal:

[O]bjects become positioned as say tables, seats, eating and drinking and serving utensils, etc. [. . .] [P]ositioned objects of the sort listed facilitate the needs of a system of human beings [. . .] sharing food together. And the set of powers of each of the objects that contributes to this end is seen as its set of functions.

(Lawson, 2012, p. 376)

In this earlier work, Lawson seems to suggest that functions are located in the causal capacities of positioned items:

[I]n describing the properties of any particular object the primary focus is very often on that subset of its causal powers that contribute to the overall workings or maintenance of the system. Indeed these causal powers tend, thereby, to be referred to as the positioned object's functions; they are looked upon according to how they function as a component of the system.

(Lawson, 2012, p. 376)

As explained earlier, through developments of the theory and the recognition that causal capacities are not always necessarily harnessed through the positioning process, Lawson has come to clarify that the functions of components of social totalities are located on the level of the positions and that functions exist whether or not they are fulfilled by the positioned items.

17 For more on Lawson's understanding of function as well as a comparison with other conceptions of function, see Pratten (2023).

18 Lawson previously tended to suggest that it was only when human persons are positioned and formed into person components that rights and obligations were involved, whereas it was when artefacts were positioned and formed into non-person components that functions were at play:

> [W]hen an *artefact* is positioned as, for example, a paperweight, traffic beacon, door or identity card, certain of its causal capacities become interpreted as its (positional) *functions*. The latter are interpreted as functions within and relative to the system in which it is positioned. However when a *human individual* is positioned as, for example, a judge or prison officer, it is not the case that capacities possessed are interpreted as functions, but rather that the individual becomes the bearer or agent of novel positional *powers* and specifically *rights and obligations*. Of course positions and positional rights and obligations are typically in place in order that certain perceived needs of the system can be met by appropriately allocated occupants. So the positioning of human beings is typically also functional. But still in the case of the positioned human individual it is rights and obligations that are acquired.
>
> (Lawson, 2014, p. 9)

If Lawson does acknowledge a "functional" element to all positioning, he draws a contrast between the formation of person components—involving rights and obligations—and the formation of non-person components—involving functions. Indeed, at times, Lawson (2015a, p. 39) has gone so far as to suggest that rights and obligations are not involved in the formation of non-person components stating that "when inanimate objects are so socially positioned, the capacities or powers most closely associated with their positioning take the form *not* of rights and obligations but of system functions". Or alternatively, Lawson writes:

> [W]ith the positioning of an artefact, rights and obligations are not obtained. Instead, certain of the artefact's causal powers become interpreted as its characteristic function set(s), according to how it indeed functions in the system(s) in which it is positioned. Thus the causal capacity of the large sea pebble placed on my desk, which becomes its positional function is that of weighing down papers, i.e., of preventing my papers from blowing about (as they otherwise might if I have the window open on a hot but breezy day).
>
> (Lawson, 2015c, p. 213)

Over time, however, Lawson has come to recognise that in the formation of community components, rights and obligations orientate the component towards serving a function that supports the overall way of working of the totality. These two features are not in contrast with one another but inextricably linked.

19 Lawson previously considered this difference in terms of contrasting positioning per se and successful positioning:

> [S]uccess is achieved only where the person or other item allocated to a position, and thereby constituting a component of a wider totality or system, is found to possess capacities that are particularly appropriate to serving the relevant function(s) of that wider totality or system and, if need be, can be continuously harnessed to this end.
>
> (Lawson, 2019b, p. 13)

Lawson has illustrated this difference in his work on money in which he has at times suggested:

> Whatever, then, is positioned as legal tender is money. Those holding it are entitled to use it as a general means of payment, as a guaranteed effective means for discharging debts held. Notice, though, that the attribution of the noted right/obligation pair does not in itself guarantee that the legal tender so formed has purchasing power. Although the legal tender must be accepted when offered for discharging an existing debt, in the UK at least, this does not guarantee that participants will enter into new debt relations with holders of money. If it is supposed that, formally, money is fully specified by identifying it with legal tender, then we have already uncovered money's nature and how it is constituted. But my concern is with a *successful* money, with properties that a money has in practice, and for this it is necessary that legal tender also possess purchasing power. In theory, a money, if interpreted just as legal tender, can exist and not possess such a power. This is the reason I distinguished a successfully functioning money from money *per se* earlier.
>
> (Lawson, 2019b, p. 159)

20 While it is not my focus here, Lawson has considered the way in which our positioning might transform the items, in this case human persons, that are positioned:

> [T]he human individual exists as a process of transformation. The structural context facing the individual makes a difference not just through enabling and constraining and facilitating certain causal powers amongst others, it also affects the very nature of human individuals. It makes a difference to the path and form of development of the capabilities, motivations and acquired needs, etc. (in short, to the formation and evolution of the nature) of a particular human being whether "he" or "she" is situated, say, as a slave or slave-owner in a slave-owning society; as a serf (freeman, villain or cottager) in European Manorialism (or Seigneurialism); as a worker or employer of modern capitalism; or indeed as a gendered man or woman at almost any time and place.
>
> (Lawson, 2012, p. 373)

21 It is important to acknowledge that Lawson (2003a, 2003b, 2007a, 2007b) has conducted extensive research pertaining to the nature of gender. This research, however, pre-dates developments to social positioning theory and the recognition of the extent to which social positioning is the central feature of the conception of social ontology developed in Cambridge. Lawson consequently characterises the nature of gender somewhat differently in such contributions to the account provided earlier. For example, Lawson writes:

> What precisely is gender [. . .]? I would define it neither as a substance, nor simply a category of analysis, but rather as a social totality, a social system. It is a system of processes and products (of processes in product and products in process). The processes in question (which are always context specific) are precisely those that work to legitimise/motivate the notion that individuals regarded as female and those regarded as male ought to be allocated to, or to have allocated to them, systematically differentiated kinds of (relationally defined) social positions. The products are the (equally transitory and spatially/culturally limited) outcomes of these processes. If the processes serve to gender, i.e. are gendering processes (or processes of genderation), the products (aspects of social relations, positions (with associated rights and norms) practices, identities) must be regarded as gendered.
>
> (Lawson, 2007a, pp. 151–152)

It is also important to recognise within the social ontology literature that there are other authors working on the nature of gender that employ the terminology—albeit in varying ways—of social position. Haslanger, for example, writes:

> Drawing on the insight that one's sex has quite well-defined and systematic social implications, feminists have argued that it is helpful to distinguish sex and gender. Very roughly, as the slogan goes, gender is the social meaning of sex. The idea is that gender is not a classification scheme based simply on anatomical or biological differences, but marks social differences between individuals. Sex differences are about testicles and ovaries, the penis and the uterus [. . .]; gender, in contrast, is a classification of individuals in terms of their social position, as determined by interpretations of their sex.
>
> (Haslanger, 2012, p. 248)

Alternatively, Witt:

> [P]ropose[s] to define the social position of being a woman and being a man in terms of the socially mediated reproductive (or engendering) functions that an individual is recognized (by others) to perform. The engendering function, like the function of providing shelter, is a relational property (an individual serves that function only in relation to other individuals). Engendering is also a function that is realized in a social context of institutions, traditions, and the like. And, like other functional properties, engendering is normative; it describes what individuals who are women and men ought to do, and not what they actually do. Women and men are responsive to and evaluable under the social role associated with their respective social positions; but the engendering function and the social roles are themselves available for normative evaluation and critique.
>
> (Witt, 2011, p. 18)

Moreover, Witt states that her:

> [P]roposal to define the social positions of being a woman and being a man in terms of their different engendering functions is far from original. This way of thinking about gender has been present in feminist theory at least since Beauvoir.
>
> (Witt, 2011, p. 42)

22 Lawson has conducted research into the nature of oppressive structures grounded in a particular conception of human flourishing:

> [H]uman beings are able to flourish and [. . .] some sets of conditions are more conducive to flourishing than others. Unlike a rock, say, that is likely indifferent to the conditions around it, human persons require more than survival and seek conditions in which they are best able to fulfil themselves *qua* human beings [. . .]. Each individual person is obviously unique in a multitude of ways, including possessing an exclusive combination of needs. But equally, human persons have various features in common, many bearing upon wellbeing. Thus, in addition to our each possessing numerous widely and frequently commented upon shared basic needs, such as for food and shelter, it is essential to our flourishing as persons that we each are also able competently to *interact or engage with* the range of forms of social and non-social being. Obvious examples of the former sort are common needs both to actualise capacities of language development and regularly to exercise language competence when acquired. Even in commonality there are always differences, however. For the manner in

which all, including any shared, capacities are actualised or developed will vary according to context. They can be conditioned by any of a range of possible factors, including age, culture, sexuality, historical paths of development and experience, generating needs in varying forms. The ethical goal, then [. . .] is a world in which we flourish in our differences.

(Lawson, 2019b, p. 226)

Oppressive structures, then, are those that impede such flourishing. Lawson has also considered how such structures might develop:

[P]rocesses of positioning and their results can manifest obstacles to flourishing in two very clear ways. Constraints on flourishing can persist because: 1) the very nature of specific positions, as manifest in the rights and obligations associated with occupancy, is inherently oppressive and/or discriminatory; and 2) individual participants, identified in some way as being of a kind, perhaps because already an occupant of a specific position, face difficulties, restrictions and discrimination when seeking to obtain entry to additional, relatively advantaged, positions (the associated tasks of which they are quite capable of successfully undertaking).

(Lawson, 2019b, p. 235)

Lawson's conception of human flourishing is grounded in an ethical framework that he refers to as Critical Ethical Naturalism. For more, see Lawson (2013, 2015b); Martins (2017) and Ragkousis (2023). For other and related perspectives, see Collier (1999) and Gorski (2013).

23 Lawson, building on his work developing Critical Ethical Naturalism, has also considered strategies for emancipatory practice:

[T]he nature of the problem that warrants emancipatory attention [. . .] is simply that the drive of each of us to flourish is repeatedly thwarted by the structures around us. Relative stability in social life consists not of patterns of events, but social structures—not least sets of positions, rights and obligations. These are the factors we draw upon in our practices, in seeking to survive, produce, create and generally go on in life. And the way these structures have been shaped by historical forces is such that many people throughout the planet continuously suffer conditions of insecurity, oppression, discrimination, bullying, poverty, limited healthcare and education opportunities, and so forth, while all of us to different degrees struggle to avoid being alienated from who we really are. In a world where there are more than adequate resources for all to flourish, the noted conditions are nevertheless maintained through the interactions of us all, in the historically determined situations in which we find ourselves, including hierarchical structures of positions, rights and obligations serving to interrelate both communities and people. The nature of existing structures and the manner in which individuals and communities are distributed to the various positions are currently far from facilitating of human flourishing. The project to consider here as an alternative to event or outcome planning, then, in its basics or fundamentals, is simply that of identifying causal structures that serve as obstacles to achieving conditions of human flourishing and thereupon seeking ways of transforming or replacing them. To pursue it, the primary emphasis and focus of critical attention must turn away from events and their hoped-for and sought-after patterns to underlying deeper structures where, as in the non-social realm, the basis of stability and continuity really lies. It is the underlying social structures, not least positional rights and obligations, that determine the shape and range of real human possibilities. The feasible goal thus becomes that of socio-structural transformation oriented to facilitating ever-greater human flourishing. How we all might act within appropriately transformed structures, and the specific events or outcomes that would thereby emerge, are matters that are unpredictable and can only unfold with time.

(Lawson, 2019b, pp. 232–233)

Lawson, then, has considered different ways in which such structural transformation can be achieved:

Prima facie, at least, three sorts of (overlapping but nevertheless distinguishable) possibilities may appear to arise in such circumstances. These are 1) to seek to transform or absent wider-scale forces in a piecemeal, step-by-step fashion, in stages, community by community; 2) to accept the operation of the harmful forces in question as inevitable and seek to harness them to facilitate a better world; and 3) to construct "local" shelters against these forces, allowing a degree of protection for some, at least for the time being.

(Lawson, 2019b, p. 235)

Lawson also acknowledges a fourth strategy. He does not include it in the list above because he thinks that it has no chance of success. Indeed, the above three constitute potential responses to its impossibility. This extra strategy involves directly addressing structures that operate at a community level when that community is transnational or, in some cases, includes the whole of humanity:

A feature of our actual world that bears significantly on possibilities for removing obstacles, albeit one that is often understated, is that very many harmful forces—though always, of course, manifest in specific/local ways in each community—operate across communities, and are often in fact transnational. Indeed, if we question in any sustained and serious way the sorts of obstacles that impact most significantly on our lives, they are seen to include the worldwide forces emanating from oppressive relations such as patriarchy and racism; the supporting structures, networks, financing and consequences of warfare; certain forms of institutionalised religion; processes of environmental degradation and pollution; prejudice and dogma in parts of the international academy; sections of the world's media in the hands of, and directed by, a powerful few, often concerned explicitly to maintain a widespread level of ignorance of various issues, not least the workings of the economy; and, of course, the operation of the economic system itself, ultimately concerned with facilitating processes of exchange and monetary accumulation or "profit" before all else. This recognition has a bearing on the appropriate level of operation of projects of social change. The latter will always be community oriented, but the level of community at which desired emancipatory change is feasible (local, national, international etc.) clearly depends on the reach and the nature of the obstacles (to generalised flourishing) that require transforming or absenting. Where it is possible to transform obstacles or harmful forces at the level at which they operate, then, a clearly appropriate strategy is to seek to do so.

(Lawson, 2019b, pp. 234–235)

More recently, Lawson (2022, p. 23) has bluntly, in relation to some oppressive structures, stated that "the obvious emancipatory way forward involves abolishing all gender, race and class positions". For more on Lawson's conception of emancipatory practice, see Lawson (2019b, Chapter 8). For a different view on the necessity of anticipation for emancipatory action from a contributor who has engaged closely with the Cambridge Social Ontology Group, see Patomäki (2018).

24 A question that is as yet unanswered is the extent to which Lawson might consider that if not all then most communities, like all individual human beings, are positioned in one way or another. I would be inclined to think so, as most communities are understood as being nested as (sub)communities of other communities, which I would understand as that community being positioned within another.

25 Previously, Lawson drew a contrast between positioning that involved function and positioning that involved rights and obligations. This was particularly apparent in early work in which Lawson contrasted the positioning of a community as an ordinary firm and the positioning of a community as a corporation:

> In the case where a community becomes positioned as an "ordinary", i.e. as an *un*incorporated, firm, a set of its capacities become interpreted as (or associated with) its (positional) *functions*. In the case where, or if, it becomes (further) positioned as a company, it acquires positional rights and obligations, just as a (positioned) human individual might. Indeed, in being so positioned it is said to acquire the status of a *legal person* (a notion I elaborate on below).
>
> (Lawson, 2014, pp. 9–10)

Over time, Lawson recognised that rights, obligations and function were all involved in community social positioning. However, it is only recently that Lawson has emphasised the vocabulary of community component formation. Previous to this, Lawson explained the positioning of communities as components of wider communities in the following terms:

> [A]ny community itself can also be so positioned, albeit in a wider community. Indeed, for a group of people to function as an ordinary business partnership, or a charity, or a school, in modern societies such as the UK, they *have to be* appropriately positioned as such. We have seen that when an artefact is positioned as, say, a traffic beacon, a chair or a certificate of some kind, with certain of its causal capacities thereby interpreted as is characteristic of a (system) function set, its use is regulated by rights and obligations that fall on human participants in the wider positioning community. And we have also seen that when, in contrast, a human individual is positioned in the community, say, as a judge or a prisoner, it is the human position occupant who becomes the agent or bearer of powers associated with that position. The question to pose, then, is: which of these models applies when it is a community that is socially positioned? In most cases, or in the first conceptual instance at least, the answer is that the positioning (registering) of the community as a firm parallels the positioning of an artefact. That is, a set of emergent powers of the community in question becomes interpreted as its characteristic function set (according to how this particular community comes to function in the wider, typically national, community), and the operations of the firm are regulated by rights and obligations born by individuals within the firm and the wider community. [. . .] However, and significantly, any such positioned community can be further positioned through a process known as incorporation. When this happens, the process instead parallels the positioning of a human individual. For in this case the community *qua* a totality acquires a set of rights and obligations.
>
> (Lawson, 2019b, pp. 131–132)

26 Take, for example, the Cambridge Social Ontology Group. The constitution of CSOG, as discussed in Chapter 1, involved a community of individuals interested in discussing ontology beginning to meet on Tuesday mornings as an additional, but more informal, meeting to the Monday night Cambridge Realist Workshop. As the group continued to meet, it eventually became useful to make things like a website and be somewhat formally considered a research group within the economics faculty of the University of Cambridge. In so doing, a non-person position

was opened up within the wider community of the economics faculty and the community of ontologically interested individuals came to occupy it, forming the non-person component CSOG. CSOG is a non-person component of the wider community because the component CSOG may not directly exercise the rights and obligations of its position. These rights and obligations, which, until recently, may have included allowing the members of the group to meet in the team room of the economics faculty on Tuesday mornings uninterrupted are, rather, accessed by the person components of the group as well as the person components of the wider community of the economics faculty who, for example, must not hold other meetings in the team room on a Tuesday morning.

Interestingly, Lawson has also at times provided communities such as CSOG as an example of a strategy for emancipatory practice involving the creation of shelters against oppressive forces which he has referred to at times as eudaimonic bubbles or communities of care. For Lawson, a community of care or eudaimonic bubble is:

> [S]imply an emergent (sub)community that is organised in a manner that participants within it are able to flourish or achieve a degree of flourishing significantly greater than that which they would otherwise be able to in the wider nesting (set of) community(ies), along at least one axis. [. . .] Familiar examples of the sort of (sub)communities I have in mind include close friendships, partnerships, many families, refuges, perhaps certain monastic communities, possibly some retreats, even [. . .] various study groups [. . .] and, fundamentally, many of those arrangements that have been set up specifically for individuals who, for some shared reason(s) (religion, skin colour, sexuality, beliefs etc.), experience regular harassment, oppression, discrimination or general negative treatment by numerous (blinkered) members of the wider, more dominant nesting community. [. . .] In all such sub-communities, interactions are, or can be, organised on the basis not of greed, exchange, opposition, oppression, unnecessary hierarchical power, dogma and suchlike, but rather of cooperation, unconditional giving, open mindedness, love and care. The aim is to avoid the worst effects of specific harms, including forms of discrimination, abuse, intellectual dogma, profiteering, harassment and so on, and instead to facilitate inclusiveness and authenticity, with resources allocated in accordance with principles of sharing and meeting needs.
>
> (Lawson, 2019b, pp. 239–240)

For Lawson, the Cambridge Social Ontology Group, operating in a hostile disciplinary context dominated by the mainstream of economics has acted as a community of care resisting such outside oppressive forces. While Lawson has considered various ways in which such communities might emerge, a facet of this process that is yet to be considered in any sustained way is the extent to which the positioning of whole communities is involved in the constitution of such eudaimonic bubbles.

27 This process, however, has a long history:

> Pope Innocent IV [. . .] used this sort of device to separate the rights and obligations of monks (who could own nothing, but could be sued for legal wrong doings) from those of their monastery (which as a legal person could own assets, but as a non-real person lacked a soul and could not therefore be negligent or excommunicated).
>
> (Lawson, 2014, p. 19)

28 For a more detailed discussion and elaboration of Lawson's account of the firm and the corporation, see Deakin (2017); Lawson (2012, 2014, 2015c, 2016b, 2016d, 2019b); Searle (2016) and Veldman and Willmott (2017).

29 Lawson underlines that, despite the terminology of legal *fiction*:

> [T]here is no ontological fiction involved here, merely a legal positioning of certain individuals as something which, without a legal interpretation, they are clearly seen not to be, in order that some outcome be achieved that could not easily be so otherwise; and specifically that rights and obligations be made available to parties for whom, in their design, they were never intended. In such cases there is always something or someone real that is repositioned. In being repositioned that something or person is not somehow rendered a fiction. To repeat, a legal fiction merely refers to a legal misrepresentation of a situation in order to allow the application of a legal rule (in particular regarding rights and obligations) to a case for which it was not originally designed or intended to cover.
>
> (Lawson, 2014, p. 19)

30 An alternative theory is that of Searle who has conceptualised the corporation as being a free standing Y term, that is, there is no X that is counted as Y:

> In the case of corporations, a pre-existing object does not become a corporation. Rather, the corporation is, so to speak, created out of nothing. And the wording of the California law for the creation of corporations makes this explicit. A corporation is created by performing a speech act: "A corporation is formed by filing articles of incorporation". Lawson tells us that there has to be a community which becomes a corporation. Why? Maybe in England a pre-existing community is required which becomes a corporation—though I doubt it—but that is not California law. California law does not state that a community becomes a corporation. Rather it states that any person, group of people, or other corporation may form a corporation entirely by performing a speech act. They do not form a corporation out of something else. They just do something—perform a speech act—that by itself forms the corporation. They do not first have to become a community, and then turn the community into a corporation. That is not how it works in California.
>
> (Searle, 2016, pp. 410–411)

Lawson argues that Searle comes up with this solution in the case of the corporation due to his inability to recognise communities as social totalities that can be so positioned:

> If Searle is to handle notions like corporations, and to recognise that they bear powers, or have status functions associated with them, it seems that he too ought to acknowledge the existence of social entities that constitute the grounding for the X term, in his X counts as Y formulation. In other words, it appears that Searle too needs to acknowledge at least some real social entities in order to be able to establish institutional facts about corporations. As it happens the corporation (on my conception) is but one example of a positioned social entity (many communities qualify). [. . .] So an interesting question to examine is how Searle make sense of these sorts of cases, all of which I take to be significant challenges to his basic conception. How does Searle deal with such examples? Searle does so not by allowing the X term in such cases to refer to emergent social entities or unobservable social structure such as power relations, but instead by relaxing the idea that there need be any X term (any object on which status functions are attached) at all [. . .].
>
> (Lawson, 2016b, p. 382)

For more on Searle's perspective and Lawson's disagreement, see Lawson (2016b, 2016d) and Searle (2010, 2016).

References

Collier, A. (1999). *Being and worth*. London and New York: Routledge.

Deakin, S. (2017). Tony Lawson's theory of the corporation: Towards a social ontology of law. *Cambridge Journal of Economics, 41*(5), 1505–1523. doi:10.1093/cje/bex044

Faulkner, P., Lawson, C., & Runde, J. (2010). Theorising technology. *Cambridge Journal of Economics, 34*(1), 1–16. doi:10.1093/cje/bep084

Faulkner, P., & Runde, J. (2009). On the identity of technological objects and user innovations in function. *The Academy of Management Review, 34*(3), 442–462. Retrieved from www.jstor.org/stable/27760013

Faulkner, P., & Runde, J. (2013). Technological objects, social positions, and the transformational model of social activity. *MIS Quarterly, 37*(3), 803–818. Retrieved from www.jstor.org/stable/43826001

Gorski, P. S. (2013). Beyond the fact/value distinction: Ethical naturalism and the social sciences. *Society, 50*(6), 543–553. doi:10.1007/s12115-013-9709-2

Haslanger, S. (2012). *Resisting reality: Social construction and social critique*. Oxford: Oxford University Press.

Ingham, G. (2018). A critique of Lawson's "Social positioning and the nature of money". *Cambridge Journal of Economics, 42*(3), 837–850. doi:10.1093/cje/bex070

Lawson, C. (2017). *Technology and isolation*. Cambridge: Cambridge University Press.

Lawson, T. (2003a). Ontology and feminist theorizing. *Feminist Economics, 9*(1), 119–150.

Lawson, T. (2003b). Theorizing ontology. *Feminist Economics, 9*(1), 161–169.

Lawson, T. (2007a). Gender and social change. In J. Browne (Ed.), *The future of gender*. Cambridge: Cambridge University Press.

Lawson, T. (2007b). Methodological issues in the study of gender. *Journal of International Economic Studies, (21)*, 1–16.

Lawson, T. (2012). Ontology and the study of social reality: Emergence, organisation, community, power, social relations, corporations, artefacts and money. *Cambridge Journal of Economics, 36*(2), 345–385. doi:10.1093/cje/ber050

Lawson, T. (2013). Ethical naturalism and forms of relativism. *Society, 50*(6), 570–575. doi:10.1007/s12115-013-9712-7

Lawson, T. (2014). The nature of the firm and peculiarities of the corporation. *Cambridge Journal of Economics, 39*(1), 1–32. doi:10.1093/cje/beu046

Lawson, T. (2015a). A conception of social ontology. In S. Pratten (Ed.), *Social ontology and modern economics* (pp. 19–52). London and New York: Routledge.

Lawson, T. (2015b). Critical ethical naturalism: An orientation to ethics. In S. Pratten (Ed.), *Social ontology and modern economics* (pp. 359–388). London and New York: Routledge.

Lawson, T. (2015c). The modern corporation: The site of a mechanism (of global social change) that is out-of-control? In M. S. Archer (Ed.), *Generative mechanisms transforming the social order* (pp. 205–231). Dordrecht: Springer.

Lawson, T. (2016a). Collective practices and norms. In M. S. Archer (Ed.), *Morphogenesis and the crisis of normativity* (pp. 249–279). Dordrecht: Springer.

Lawson, T. (2016b). Comparing conceptions of social ontology: Emergent social entities and/or institutional facts? *Journal for the Theory of Social Behaviour, 46*(4), 359–399. doi:10.1111/jtsb.12126

Lawson, T. (2016c). Social positioning and the nature of money. *Cambridge Journal of Economics, 40*(4), 961–996. doi:10.1093/cje/bew006

Lawson, T. (2016d). Some critical issues in social ontology: Reply to John Searle. *Journal for the Theory of Social Behaviour, 46*(4), 426–437.

Lawson, T. (2018a). The constitution and nature of money. *Cambridge Journal of Economics, 42*(3), 851–873. doi:10.1093/cje/bey005

Lawson, T. (2018b). Debt as money. *Cambridge Journal of Economics*, 42(4), 1165–1181. doi:10.1093/cje/bey006

Lawson, T. (2019a). Money's relation to debt: Some problems with MMT's conception of money. *Real-World Economics Review*, (89), 109–128.

Lawson, T. (2019b). *The nature of social reality: Issues in social ontology*. London and New York: Routledge.

Lawson, T. (2022). Social positioning theory. *Cambridge Journal of Economics*, 46(1), 1–39. doi:10.1093/cje/beab040

Martins, N. O. (2017). Critical ethical naturalism and the transformation of economics. *Cambridge Journal of Economics*, 41(5), 1323–1342. doi:10.1093/cje/bex036

Patomäki, H. (2018). Reflexivity of anticipations in economics and political economy. In R. Poli (Ed.), *Handbook of anticipation: Theoretical and applied aspects of the use of future in decision making* (pp. 1–26). Cham: Springer International Publishing.

Pratten, S. (2023). The concept of function in social positioning theory. *Journal for the Theory of Social Behaviour*, 53(4), 560–582. doi:https://doi.org/10.1111/jtsb.12389

Ragkousis, A. (2023). Aristotelian themes in critical ethical naturalism. *Cambridge Journal of Economics*. doi:10.1093/cje/bead014

Searle, J. R. (1995). *The construction of social reality*. London: Penguin.

Searle, J. R. (2010). *Making the social world: The structure of human civilization*. Oxford: Oxford University Press.

Searle, J. R. (2016). The limits of emergence: Reply to Tony Lawson. *Journal for the Theory of Social Behaviour*, 46(6), 400–412. doi:10.1111/jtsb.12125

Searle, J. R. (2017). Money: Ontology and deception. *Cambridge Journal of Economics*, 41(5), 1453–1470. doi:10.1093/cje/bex034

Veldman, J., & Willmott, H. (2017). Social ontology and the modern corporation. *Cambridge Journal of Economics*, 41(5), 1489–1504. doi:10.1093/cje/bex043

Witt, C. (2011). *The metaphysics of gender*. Oxford: Oxford University Press.

Index

Printed in the United States
by Baker & Taylor Publisher Services